To:

_____

God will yet fill your mouth
with laughter.

Job 8:21

From:

_____

Laughter for a Woman's Soul
Copyright © 2001 by New Life Clinics
ISBN 0-310-97795-9

Requests for information should be addressed to:
Inspirio, The Gift Group of Zondervan
Grand Rapids, Michigan 49530
http://www.inspiriogifts.com

Associate Editor: Molly Detweiler
Project Editor: Sarah M. Hupp
Art Director: Amy E. Langeler
Designer: Amy Peterman
Illustrations: Lyn Boyer

Printed in China

03 04 / HK/ 5

Laughter FOR A WOMAN'S SOUL

Revive Your Spirit with Women of Faith

inspirio

The gift group of Zondervan

Table of Contents

Part III: Laughter Is Good Medicine

Part IV: Laughter Is Contagious

Because of Jesus

I couldn't help myself. I remembered some of the stories Luci, Patsy, Marilyn, Barbara, and Thelma tell when they speak at the conferences, and I started to laugh. I was recalling Luci's story about the Chihuahua in which Luci, as the loser of a bet with Marilyn, had to go up to a stranger and tell her that her Chihuahua was so much better and to thank her for her prayers. Then there's Luci's story about the time she put the name Bernadette Apes down on the visitor's card in a small neighborhood church, not realizing that the pastor would call out her name from the pulpit and attempt to engage her in conversation.

These wonderful women have brought so much joy and friendship to me. Christ is enough for all of us. His loving acceptance of us enables us to accept ourselves and others. With that as a beginning point, we can relax, be ourselves, and connect with others who have discovered the joy of just being themselves—flawed and silly but of worth because of Jesus.

© SHEILA WALSH

A sticker that covers those holes in the top of the cleanser can caught my attention. It was so full of "stick-um," it seemed a waste to toss it into the trash. Carrying it into the bedroom, I placed the sticker inside my husband Ken's pant leg.

The next day, Ken wore the slacks I had "stickered" but said nothing about it. I was dying of curiosity, but didn't ask.

Weeks later I was speaking at a luncheon and became aware of an irritation in my right armpit. No amount of subtle movement seemed to bring relief. At home, I discovered the sticker in the underarm portion of my blouse.

This game went on for weeks. Finally, Ken announced that the sticker had no more "stick-um." Only then did we settle into a raucous description of our experiences with the sticker.

Adults assume that being playful might be interpreted as being childish. Jesus said it's impossible to enter the kingdom unless we become as little children. A childlike spirit is capable of fascination, wonder, and enthusiasm. Revel in that simplicity.

MARILYN MEBERG

Promises About Childlike Laughter

Our mouths were filled with laughter, our tongues with songs of joy. Then it was said among the nations, "The LORD has done great things for them."

Psalm 126:2

God has brought me laughter.

Genesis 21:6

Jesus said, "Blessed are you who weep now, for you will laugh."

Luke 6:21

Jesus said, "Let the little children come to me, and do not hinder them, for the kingdom of God belongs to such as these. I tell you the truth, anyone who will not receive the kingdom of God like a little child will never enter it."

Mark 10:14-15

God's Gifts Beget Giggles

I wonder what exclamation escaped Adam when he saw his first rhino, baboon, and ostrich. I bet if he had had a horn, he would have honked it that day. Imagine the magnificent view the first couple must have had of the firmament without the distraction and diffusion of city lights and pollution.

Our God is a gift giver. His generosity is obvious in how lavishly he bestows on us rainbows, waterfalls, canyons, and white caps. The Lord serves up his scrumptious beauty in liberal portions and then invites us to partake. His voilas turn into wonderment for me.

As the sun sets, the mountains go through a series of thrilling changes. From pinks to lavenders to deep purples, the setting sun and emerging evening appear to cover the hillside for sleep. Marilyn and I never tire of the Lord's thrilling displays. We ooh and ah in all the right places. Smiles and giggles of pleasure help us to express our gratitude. And we, like Adam, would honk if we had a horn.

© PATSY CLAIRMONT

*L*uci, two dear friends, and I flew to Chile for what proved to be an off-the-charts, fantastic trip. I was really hyped, but I wasn't prepared for the utter delight I felt as our bus made its way down to the coastal penguin rookery.

As we exited the bus, we stood literally knee-high in penguins. Some awkwardly headed for the ocean where they fell in while others milled about. One particularly friendly penguin turned to a woman and began an energetic effort to loosen her shoelaces. When the shoelaces would not yield, the penguin pummeled the woman's leg with a succession of flipper slaps that sent us all into hysterics.

To my knowledge, penguins don't serve any useful purpose in life other than to give people like me immense pleasure. Perhaps God put together some things in life for no other reason than that we might "sing for joy at the works of his hands." From the grandeur of snow-capped peaks to the awkward land inefficiency of penguins, what fun it is simply to "sing for joy" about his creation.

© MARILYN MEBERG

Promises About
God's Gifts

The LORD God is a sun and shield; the LORD bestows favor and honor; no good thing does he withhold from those whose walk is blameless.

❧ Psalm 84:11

Every good and perfect gift is from above, coming down from the Father of the heavenly lights, who does not change like shifting shadows.

❧ James 1:17

We have different gifts, according to the grace given us.

❧ Romans 12:6

You do not lack any spiritual gift as you eagerly wait for our Lord Jesus Christ to be revealed.

❧ 1 Corinthians 1:7

With Love and Rejoicing

*U*ncle Hugh sat by the fire and refused to come to the table with the rest of us, so he was served where it was warm and cozy. When Uncle Hugh turned on the television, my aunt was mortified. Not only was it Sunday, when watching television was frowned upon, but also her dad had turned on horse racing!

My grandmother managed to negotiate a compromise. Uncle Hugh could watch the race if he turned off the sound. With this treaty signed, Uncle Pete launched into a lengthy grace. Halfway through his prayer, a voice from across the room bellowed, "Look at that one with the white legs!"

No one dared to breathe. Then my mother almost fell off her chair with laughter. We all laughed until the tears rolled off our cheeks.

God's love can make you forget yourself at times, just like Uncle Hugh. You can run in out of the cold, sit by the fire, put up your feet, and just be yourself. You are loved, you are loved, you are loved—even with white legs!

© SHEILA WALSH

My husband and I decided to obtain a credit card. I began to avail myself of its generosity. Ken mentioned the overuse of the card to me several times. But ...

One morning I opened the door to a stern-looking gentleman. He asked if he could see my Bank of America card. I mindlessly handed it to him. He pulled from his pocket a small pair of scissors, sliced the card in two, and handed the pieces back to me. Turning on his heel he said, "That's what happens to card abusers!"

Slowly, the scenario began to make sense. I started to grin, giggle, and finally guffaw.

Ken made me laugh. At least once a day he would whiplash me with giggle inspirations. He gave me a birthday present in a huge box that progressed down to a tiny box. In the tiny box was a charm for my bracelet. Guess what it was? A small pair of scissors.

Our rejoicing over one another was a sweet gift. I'm grateful. But God's rejoicing over us is even sweeter. What a God!

© MARILYN MEBERG

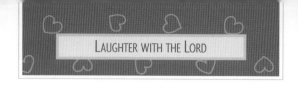
Promises About God's Love & Rejoicing

The LORD your God is with you, he is mighty to save. He will take great delight in you, he will quiet you with his love, he will rejoice over you with singing.

Zephaniah 3:17

The LORD delights in those who fear him, who put their hope in his unfailing love.

Psalm 147:11

The LORD takes delight in his people; he crowns the humble with salvation.

Psalm 149:4

The LORD will take delight in you.

Isaiah 62:4

He's Looking at You

❧

"I volunteered to sing at the local nursing home this past Sunday," she began. "I wanted to bring a little joy to the residents who don't get out much."

"Well, six people showed up. Three ladies fell asleep before I started. Another was off in a corner dancing to a tune that was different from the one I was singing, but the loudest one of all sat right up front, just under my nose. Her hearing aid was turned up too high, and it was giving off high-pitched whining noises. Every time I began another song she cried out at the top of her lungs, 'Oh, no, she's going to sing again!'"

Do you ever feel as if no one seems to notice or appreciate you? God sees our hearts, and that's all he cares about. He doesn't miss a single moment of a life lived out for him. If everyone in your audience has dozed off or danced off to another tune, you might want to check again. There, in the corner, is God, watching and listening and appreciating you.

© SHEILA WALSH

A little boy ran to the sidelines after try-outs for the soccer team and told his mother, "Mom, I guess I'm better than I thought; the coaches must have heard of me. They just called everyone else by his number, but they kept calling me by name!"

His mother didn't have the heart to point out to him that he was the only one with his name imprinted above the number on the back of his shirt. But we don't have to worry that God won't know us. He has known us—each one of us—since he knit us together in our mothers' wombs (Psalm 139:13).

He knows us by name (Isaiah 43:1), and he'll never stumble over the pronunciation or forget who we are. He wears our names on his hands (Isaiah 49:16).

And we can be assured that he knows more than just our names; he knows all about us (Psalm 139:3)—and loves us anyway!

© BARBARA JOHNSON

Promises About God
Knowing Us

O LORD, you have searched me and you know me. You know when I sit and when I rise; you perceive my thoughts from afar.

 Psalm 139:1-2

The LORD declared, "Before I formed you in the womb I knew you, before you were born I set you apart."

 Jeremiah 1:5

The man who loves God is known by God.

 1 Corinthians 8:3

"I have engraved you on the palms of my hands," says the LORD.

 Isaiah 49:16

Trust Only in Him

❧

When we're very young, we're full of excitement about all our "firsts"—our first steps, our first day of school! If we're surrounded by faith-filled adults, then we get the message, "Get ready for the exciting and wonderful time you'll have watching and participating in the events of your life!" But most of us don't get that message, do we? Instead we're warned, "Don't get your hopes up. Don't expect too much—you'll only be disappointed."

When our minds start swinging from one negative thought to another like an acrobat flying from one trapeze to the next, we find ourselves in danger of falling. Yet Jesus is always beneath us, waiting to catch us. He's our only real H.O.P.E.

H: Heavenly.
O: Omnipotent.
P: Powerful.
E: Everlasting Savior.

When we trust in him alone, life may still shake us up, but our spirit will be safe in his love.

© THELMA WELLS

$\mathcal{E}$ver wish you could start over? Probably all of us have longed for another chance in some area of our lives. We wouldn't necessarily have done things differently, just more or perhaps less.

The truth is we can't go back, only forward into uncharted territory. To sit in our sorrow would lead to misery. Although regret that leads to change is a dear friend, regret that leads to shame is a treacherous enemy.

So how do we live without allowing regret to rob us of our joy? How about this insight to prompt us on: "Lean not on your own understanding" (Proverbs 3:5).

Sometimes we are so certain we know something, when, dear sisters, we don't really. Know what I mean? There is no guarantee that if we had done a part of our lives differently things would end up any different. We have to trust the God of the universe who directs the outcome of all things that he will do that which ultimately needs to be done (in spite of us, if necessary).

© PATSY CLAIRMONT

Promises About Trusting God

Those who know your name will trust in you, for you, LORD, have never forsaken those who seek you.

 Psalm 9:10

Trust in the LORD forever, for the LORD, the LORD, is the Rock eternal.

 Isaiah 26:4

Fear of man will prove to be a snare, but whoever trusts in the LORD is kept safe.

 Proverbs 29:25

The LORD is good, a refuge in times of trouble. He cares for those who trust in him.

 Nahum 1:7

He who trusts in the LORD will prosper.

 Proverbs 28:25

Watching Closely

In Britain, an evangelist or singer would never stay in a hotel after an evening meeting. Hospitality would be extended from a member of the local church. I remember staying with an old lady in Bristol, England, who had forty-three cats. I like cats, but forty-three are too many for me. I drank my cup of cocoa with cat fur in it, and then headed to bed.

Fluffy, Muffy, and the gang made themselves comfortable on the bed, in my suitcase, and in my toilet bag. As I went to sleep I prayed, "Lord, please keep these beasts off me while I'm sleeping."

I woke up to find I was suffocating. I was drowning ... no, it was worse than that. "Help, Lord, there's a cat on my face!"

Is it hard for you to close your eyes at night? Do you worry about what tomorrow will hold? Psalm 121 makes it clear God never closes his eyes. He is always watching over you ... even if you have fur in your mouth.

© SHEILA WALSH

At times we experience the sweetness of God's nearness and at other times the frightening loneliness of his distance. The Lord hasn't changed locations, but we might have become caught up in our own agendas and forgotten his presence and availability.

Other times the Lord will be silently still (scary) for holy purposes (awesome) we don't understand (frustrating).

Perhaps we need to rest from our pursuit of the Almighty and allow him to reveal himself to us. He is in our prayers guiding our words, he is in our songs as we worship him, and he is filling our mouths when we comfort a friend or speak wisdom to someone who needs hope.

Sometimes we can search so hard for the miraculous, we miss the obvious reality of his ever-present nearness. Count your blessings. He is in them, too.

When our hearts are tenderly responsive and it suits his greater plan, then the Lord will lift the thin veil that separates us. We will be stunned to realize that he has been closer than our own breath all along.

© PATSY CLAIRMONT

Promises About God's
Watchful Care

The LORD will keep you from all harm—he will watch over your life; the LORD will watch over your coming and going both now and forevermore.

 Psalm 121:7-8

Jesus said, "Look at the birds of the air; they do not sow or reap or store away in barns, and yet your heavenly Father feeds them. Are you not much more valuable than they?"

 Matthew 6:26

Cast all your anxiety on God because he cares for you.

 1 Peter 5:7

The LORD will not let your foot slip—he who watches over you will not slumber.

 Psalm 121:3

Focus on God

The last time I ordered new glasses I had no-glare coating put on the lenses. That way, when I'm speaking, I don't reflect light like some kind of Star Wars invader every time I turn my head. That no-glare stuff really works great, but there is a side effect—my lenses smudge easily. I'm constantly viewing life through thumbprints, which eliminates a lot of life's little details like steps, curbs, and hedges.

People even offer to clean my glasses for me. How embarrassing. Their efforts only seem to rearrange the design of the smudges. I'm constantly asked, "How do you see through them?" I guess I've adjusted to people looking like walking trees.

To see clearly could be more of a reality check than I'm ready for. We resist looking honestly at our lives. We need to change our lenses so we might not only see others and ourselves more accurately, but also lift our eyes and focus on God.

© Patsy Clairmont

$\mathcal{I}$n the wee hours of my childhood mornings when I would come, sleepy-eyed, from my bedroom, there would be my mother, in prayer or Bible study. That picture of her sitting on her bed is impressed on my mind forever. In one hand she'd have her Bible and in the other, a notebook—or as she called it, "My Promise Book." Mother kept a record in that book of what God was teaching her, people she was praying for, issues she was concerned about, neighbors she wanted to see come to Christ. Every day she journaled her thoughts, feelings, God's promises to her, the words to hymns she found encouraging, poetry, and prayers. Mother's notebooks were a tremendous encouragement to her faith. Now, many years later, they are an encouragement to me.

If you have never journaled, don't be intimidated. Start where you are. Give it a try. Get a notebook. Take some time. See what happens. I think you'll surprise yourself with what comes out of your heart.

© LUCI SWINDOLL

Promises About Focusing on God

Whatever is true, whatever is noble, whatever is right, whatever is pure, whatever is lovely, whatever is admirable—if anything is excellent or praise worthy—think about such things. Whatever you have learned or received or heard from me, or seen in me—put it into practice. And the God of peace will be with you.

 Philippians 4:8-9

"I will put my laws in their minds and write them on their hearts. I will be their God, and they will be my people," says the Lord.

 Hebrews 8:10

Set your minds on things above, not on earthly things. ... When Christ, who is your life, appears, then you also will appear with him in glory.

 Colossians 3:2, 4

Our Caring, Heavenly Father

You've heard of right-brained and left-brained. Well, I'm bird-brained. No, not in regard to my cranial capacity but referring to my love for winged creatures. A portion of my brain takes great delight in the flight and fancy of birds.

My all-time favorite feathered friend would have to be the bluebird. If you ever see the sunlight reflect off their feathers, your heart will take flight. Bluebirds love open fields and fence posts. They aren't seed eaters; so to draw them into country yards takes birdhouses (mounted on fence posts) and birdbaths.

Matthew tells us, "Look at the birds of the air; they do not sow or reap or store away in barns, and yet your heavenly Father feeds them. Are you not much more valuable than they?" (Matthew 6:26). Our heavenly Father provides for the birds. What a lovely thought; he, too, is a bird-watcher. And to think his care and provision for us is even greater, for he is a people watcher, too. How comforting.

© PATSY CLAIRMONT

Daddy gave me tangible gifts, and many intangible ones as well. I received letters from him every week. The letters were laced with love, encouragement from God's Word, and profound understanding of me—not only as his daughter, but also as a person. He had my best interest at heart all the time. By his lavish giving, unconditional love, and awareness of my deepest needs, Daddy was all the cheering squad I ever needed. Because of him, I had an excellent model of a gracious, caring heavenly Father.

Although we don't all have that kind of earthly model of love and affection, everybody who is a child of God has a heavenly Father who exceeds all expectations and imagination. My dad seemed like the ringleader of our home, but the reason he was such a great parent was he knew the true Ringleader intimately. It was my father's relationship with Christ that made him such a quality person. Each of us who knows Christ personally can relate to a perfect heavenly Father and become more like him every day.

© LUCI SWINDOLL

Promises About Our Caring Heavenly Father

Jesus said, "Do not worry, saying, 'What shall we eat?' or 'What shall we drink?' or 'What shall we wear?' ... Your heavenly Father knows that you need them. But seek first his kingdom and his righteousness, and all these things will be given to you as well."

 Matthew 6:31-33

Jesus said, "Whoever acknowledges me before men, I will also acknowledge him before my Father in heaven."

 Matthew 10:32

He is our God and we are the people of his pasture, the flock under his care.

 Psalm 95:7

God will cover you with his feathers, and under his wings you will find refuge; his faithfulness will be your shield and rampart.

 Psalm 91:4

Let Go, and Let God

The very day I released my first book, *Capture Your Audience Through Storytelling,* another publisher approached me about writing my second book. I was startled. Write another book? I didn't think I had anything else to say. The publisher said, "I want you to write about the challenges and triumphs of your life."

One of the administrators at New Life Clinics read the book and was convinced I needed to be a Women of Faith speaker—me, a person she had never met or heard of. No coincidence!

I was fifty-two years old when I wrote my first book. Now, at fifty-seven, I have either written or coauthored six books. This writing frenzy all started with a friend suggesting me as a speaker for a conference. And the "coincidences" go on.

As you look back over the circumstances of your life, can you discern the carefully planned patterns that at first looked like coincidences? Situations don't always follow our plans, but God orchestrates our lives nonetheless— sometimes to a tune we hear only faintly.

© THELMA WELLS

Last week I was in the grocery store and there was a mother and her little son in front of me, pushing their cart along.

This kid was driving me crazy with his constant demands: "Let me hold that. Let me push the cart. Let me ride up there. Let me have the cookies. Let me pay the money."

Let! That's one of the most powerful words in the English language. It urges consent. As I drove home from the store, I kept thinking about that word, and realized it is used repeatedly in the Bible. I took time to check out some of the references and found that the "let verses" cover practically every mandate in the Christian life.

Listen to a few:

1 John 4:7	Let us love one another.
Hebrews 12:2	Let us fix our eyes on Jesus.
Colossians 4:6	Let your conversation be always full of grace.

Do a personal Bible study on this simple, wonderful, powerful word. Look up the verse, meditate on it, and ask God to make it real in your life.

© LUCI SWINDOLL

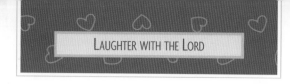
Promises About Letting God

The mind controlled by the Spirit is life and peace.

 Romans 8:6

The plans of the LORD stand firm forever, the purposes of his heart through all generations.

 Psalm 33:11

Commit to the LORD whatever you do, and your plans will succeed.

 Proverbs 16:3

He's Always Listening

✿

On a beautiful April day in Dallas, I looked up toward the heavens. Not a cloud was in the sky. But something grabbed my attention—lines of wires laced together in conduits swagged from tall poles. These masses of wires make it possible for us to talk with our friends via telephone, e-mail, fax, and telegraph.

When it storms, and these cables are down ... we can't call for help. We can't send a message to anyone.

Yet nothing can keep you from being directly connected to God if you want to be. It doesn't matter what time of day or night it is; who else is talking to him; or what the problem is. When you need to make decisions and nobody on earth understands, call him up. When your problems seem unbearable, call him up. When you want to praise him and show appreciation for his wonderful work in your life, call him up.

It doesn't matter if the telephone lines are down all over the world, God is always available.

© THELMA WELLS

At the call center in Denver International Airport, there's the Forbidden Name List, a computer compilation of names with hidden meanings that the operators are instructed not to broadcast. For example, you will not hear this page at the Denver airport: "Ms. Bath, Ms. Anita Bath." Nor will you hear, "Mr. Dover, Mr. Ben Dover" or "Ms. Popp, Ms. Lolly Popp."

Sometimes, though, a caller slips one over on the wary operators. That happened last summer, when a page rang out through the airport for "Mr. Dopolina, Mr. Bob Dopolina." Thousands of passengers could sing along with the rest of the tune, "Bobdopolina-da-bop-bam-boom!"

When I read about these relayed messages, I chuckled, but then I thought of how fortunate we are that when we need to get an urgent message to our Father in heaven, we don't have to route our plea through a busy call center. Isaiah 58:9 promises, "Then you will call, and the LORD will answer."

© BARBARA JOHNSON

Promises About God Always Listening

You will call, and the LORD will answer; you will cry for help, and he will say: Here am I.

 Isaiah 58:9

Jesus said, "Ask and it will be given to you; seek and you will find; knock and the door will be opened to you. For everyone who asks receives; he who seeks finds; and to him who knocks, the door will be opened."

 Matthew 7:7-8

The LORD said, "You will call upon me and come and pray to me, and I will listen to you."

 Jeremiah 29:12

"Before they call I will answer; while they are still speaking I will hear," says the LORD.

 Isaiah 65:24

God Made You—You!

*G*od made you an original; don't die a copy. In Christ, you can be the best of what and who you want to BEE!

According to aeronautical science, the bumblebee can't fly. Its body is too heavy, and its wings are too shallow. But the bumblebee doesn't know it can't fly. So it flies around doing what God chose for it to do, pollinating plants. It does so without considering its limitations.

You, too, have talent, skill, aptitude, and ability that are you-niquely yours. We can be the best of what and who we want to BEE—and only God knows what our limitations are.

You might appear to be different—or even strange—to some people. But remember, God made you in his image for his glory. Use your uniqueness to edify people and glorify God. Capitalize on the abilities God has given you. Don't expect other people to be like you or to always understand you. They're busy being uniquely themselves.

© THELMA WELLS

I've never had an identity crisis. Nonetheless, I'm constantly clarifying who I am. The conversation goes like this:

"I love your husband. I listen to him on *Insight for Living*."

"He's my brother."

With obvious disappointment and disillusionment, "But I thought you were his wife."

Feeling sympathetic, I apologize. "I'm sorry. I'm not married to him."

With utter frustration, "But, why not? I told my friends you were his wife."

Please! I love the guy dearly, but I'm definitely not Chuck's wife.

So who am I? Me. I'm myself. No other. No duplicate. No clone. Luci Swindoll—me.

Psalm 100:3 says, "Know that the LORD is God. It is he who made us, and we are his."
That pretty much settles it for me. Always has. He created me, and I'm who he wants me to be. Nothing more. Nothing less. Nothing else. That's true for you, as well.

LUCI SWINDOLL

Promises About Your Uniqueness

God created man in his own image, in the image of God he created him; male and female he created them.

 Genesis 1:27

We are God's workmanship, created in Christ Jesus to do good works, which God prepared in advance for us to do.

 Ephesians 2:10

I praise you, LORD, because I am fearfully and wonderfully made; your works are wonderful, I know that full well.

 Psalm 139:14

The LORD says, "Fear not, for I have redeemed you; I have summoned you by name; you are mine."

 Isaiah 43:1

God's Outrageous Love

There is nothing average about the God we know, the Father we long to serve.
He's unconventional and exorbitant.
He's extravagant in his giving. He's unrestrained in his love for us. In fact, God is extraordinary in every way. He's outrageous! If you and I were to catch even a glimpse of who he is, our lives would never be the same. And yet, he's shown us who he is. His truth and glory are revealed in his Son, Jesus Christ. And we see it every day in the universe he created, in the lives of others, and in our own experience. We often miss it, but it's there. We just forget to notice. The joy he provides is outrageous because it is completely unencumbered by the circumstances we face.

Let's notice. Let's pay careful attention. Let's let our everyday lives be invaded and transformed by this loving, gracious, wonderful, perfectly outrageous God.

© LUCI SWINDOLL

$\mathcal{I}$'m learning a lot about God's character from my little boy.

It had just stopped raining when Christian and I walked across the mall parking lot to the car. Now the sun was shining, causing steam to rise from the sticky asphalt. A hundred yards from our car was a large puddle. We walked up to it and stopped at the edge. Christian looked at me and I looked at him and then at our white summer shoes. As one soul we both jumped into the puddle at the same time and splashed and splashed until little drops of water ran down our legs and onto our now muddy shoes.

That's how the outrageous message of the love of God affects me. You see, experiencing God's love and loving him in return is not just about living a good life. It's not just about duty or obedience. It's about loving with abandon. It's knowing he's still there when everyone else has left.

© SHEILA WALSH

Promises About God's Outrageous Love

*G*od so loved the world that he gave his one and only Son, that whoever believes in him shall not perish but have eternal life.

 John 3:16

*T*he LORD said, "I have loved you with an everlasting love; I have drawn you with loving-kindness."

 Jeremiah 31:3

*K*now therefore that the LORD your God is God; he is the faithful God, keeping his covenant of love to a thousand generations of those who love him and keep his commands.

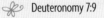 Deuteronomy 7:9

*G*od demonstrates his own love for us in this: While we were still sinners, Christ died for us.

 Romans 5:8

43

The Touch of God's Love

God loved the world so tenderly
His only Son he gave,
That all who on His Name believe
Its wondrous power will save.

For God so loved the world that He gave his only Son,
That whosoever believeth in Him
Should not perish, should not perish;
That whosoever believeth in Him
Should not perish, but have everlasting life.

Oh, love that only God can feel,
And only He can show!
Its height and depth,
Its length and breadth
Nor heav'n nor earth can know!

For God so loved the world that He gave his only Son,
That whosoever believeth in Him
Should not perish, should not perish;
That whosoever believeth in Him
Should not perish, but have everlasting life.

O Savior, melt these hearts of ours,
And teach us to believe
That whosoever comes to Thee
Shall endless life receive.

© FANNY CROSBY

Do you enjoy hearing tender words from your spouse, children, family, and friends? Of course you do. However, to know that we are loved by an omnipotent, omnipresent, omniscient Lord is the grandest feeling of acceptance anyone can have. When other people fail to express their love to us, we can always depend on Jesus.

Imagine Jesus himself saying to you:

"Child of mine, I love you with an everlasting love. I love you with unconditional love. I love you because I want to! I love you when others think you are unlovable. I love you when you have sinned and come short of my glory. I love you in the good times and in the bad."

© THELMA WELLS

Promises About the Touch of God's Love

I pray that you, being rooted and established in love, may have power, together with all the saints, to grasp how wide and long and high and deep is the love of Christ, and to know this love that surpasses knowledge—that you may be filled to the measure of all the fullness of God.

 Ephesians 3:17-19

This is love: not that we loved God, but that he loved us and sent his Son as an atoning sacrifice for our sins.

 1 John 4:10

Because of his great love for us, God, who is rich in mercy, made us alive with Christ even when we were dead in transgressions—it is by grace you have been saved. And God raised us up with Christ and seated us with him in the heavenly realms in Christ Jesus, in order that in the coming ages he might show the incomparable riches of his grace, expressed in his kindness to us in Christ Jesus.

 Ephesians 2:4-7

God's Great Gift of Grace

Grace is not meant for only special occasions. I still tease my mom about her "good" clothes. When she buys a new suit or dress, it will hang in her wardrobe for eons, waiting for just the right occasion. I, on the other hand, most often try to squeeze into a new outfit in the car on my way home from the store. God's grace is not a suit meant for Sundays; we should wrap it around our shoulders every day of our lives.

Can you imagine how the world would be transformed if we all chose to live with gracious, generous hearts? This kind of living would transform everything it came in contact with. There is no better moment to pour your love out on another: *Carpe diem*: Seize the day!

© SHEILA WALSH

Starting a day with laughter is my thing. Some years ago when I awakened from a dream, laughing, I was delighted.

I dreamed somebody in a white robe presented me with a gift-wrapped box. I opened it, but the only thing inside was a smaller box. So I opened it. Yet another box was there, smaller still. This went on box after box. ... Each box had been beautifully wrapped, but was empty.

I turned to the white-robed figure and said, "There's nothing in the boxes."

He replied, "The gifts are there. Keep looking."

There just might be a parallel between that dream and my life as a believer in Jesus Christ. At the moment we receive Christ as Savior, he presents us with his biggest gift of all: salvation by his grace. Inside that beautiful box are other gifts from the Lord—all by-products of grace. With the human eye they can't be seen or touched, but they are real, nonetheless. Don't be duped into thinking that because you don't see it, grace isn't there. It is. Keep looking.

© LUCI SWINDOLL

Promises About Grace

From the fullness of God's grace we have all received one blessing after another.

 John 1:16

All are justified freely by God's grace through the redemption that came by Christ Jesus.

 Romans 3:24

Since we have been justified through faith, we have peace with God through our LORD Jesus Christ, through whom we have gained access by faith into this grace in which we now stand. And we rejoice in the hope of the glory of God.

 Romans 5:1-2

God is able to make all grace abound to you, so that in all things at all times, having all that you need, you will abound in every good work.

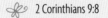 2 Corinthians 9:8

God's Love Is Life-changing

$\mathcal{G}$od's love is a gift that can make you forget yourself at times. The Scottish writer George MacDonald said, "It is the heart that is not yet sure of its God that is afraid to laugh in his presence."

So often with old people and children all sense of what would be appropriate is swallowed up in what feels right. That's refreshing. We waste too many years between childhood and our older years measuring our behavior on a scale we think we see in someone else's eyes.

God loves us as we are right now! That's one of the things I'm most grateful for. I love the freedom to be myself in God. I pray that a year from now, five years from now, I will be a godlier woman, but I know God won't love me any more than he does right this minute.

© SHEILA WALSH

As a little girl I'd run home from school during blustery Michigan winters. I remember the crunch of snow under my galoshes as I ran up the steps. Inside, the tantalizing aroma of my mother's homemade soup enfolded me. I'd warm up by the heating grate in the floor, feeling the whoosh of warm air all around me.

Use the fuel of God's love to turn trouble into heat and energy for yourself and other people. Stoke the smoldering embers of your passion for life. As the smoke curls from the chimney, other people will be drawn to the sweet aroma of compassion.

© BARBARA JOHNSON

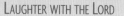

Promises About God's Life-changing Love

God is love. Whoever lives in love lives in God, and God in him.

 1 John 4:16

Love is patient, love is kind. It does not envy, it does not boast, it is not proud. It is not rude, it is not self-seeking, it is not easily angered, it keeps no record of wrongs. Love does not delight in evil but rejoices with the truth. It always protects, always trusts, always hopes, always perseveres. Love never fails.

 1 Corinthians 13:4-8

We, who with unveiled faces all reflect the Lord's glory, are being transformed into his likeness with ever-increasing glory, which comes from the Lord, who is the Spirit.

 2 Corinthians 3:18

God's Grace Brings Joy

❀

The wonderful and outrageous thing about grace is that you get to be Mary or Martha, and if you really understand grace, both bring joy. That was one of the hardest lessons for me to learn. I thought that what I did for God and others made me loved, but I was really fed up with it. Now I understand that I am loved by God anyway, even if I do stay under the bed for a couple of months. So I enjoy most of my busy days, and when I get a day like today I make a cup of tea, sit down with Christian, and watch the Barney movie for the nine hundredth time.

You see, when you really "get it," really understand that God's grace is enough and will always be there, then you can spin plates, juggle melons, and sing the "Hallelujah Chorus"—all four parts, all at the same time. And you'll be sure that God's grace is sufficient even if a few of those melons splatter on the ground!

© SHEILA WALSH

Sheila wears the most outrageous high-heeled shoes. How high are they? Well, let's just say I climbed into them one day, and my ears began to pop and I developed a nosebleed.

Sheila often walks—sometimes even skips—in these heels to the extreme edge of the platform while speaking, allowing the toes of her shoes to hang off the stage. Luci, Marilyn, Thelma, Barbara, and I, who are seated five steps below the platform, gasp as we go into full-body alert, ready to throw ourselves forward if she should topple. That hasn't happened ... yet. But we are willing to respond if our cohort should need our help.

Isn't that a tiny picture of what grace is all about? The Lord is there for us when we need him most and possibly deserve his involvement least. It also encompasses those times when we think we can't take the next scary step. God gives us the grace to let go and inch forward in baby increments, or sometimes even skip like a gazelle.

© PATSY CLAIRMONT

Promises About God's Grace & Joy

*I*n Christ we have redemption through his blood, the forgiveness of sins, in accordance with the riches of God's grace

 Ephesians 1:7

*M*ay all who seek you rejoice and be glad in you; may those who love your salvation always say, "Let God be exalted!"

 Psalm 70:4

*T*he ransomed of the LORD will return. They will enter Zion with singing; everlasting joy will crown their heads. Gladness and joy will overtake them, and sorrow and sighing will flee away.

 Isaiah 51:11

Common Pots & Odd Ducks

*G*od does his extraordinary work through common, ordinary people. Our society puts an inordinate emphasis upon external success and being number one.

That doesn't seem to matter a whit to God. Jesus used ordinary flowers, trees, and birds to teach profound lessons about himself and about life. He placed ordinary mud from the ground on the eyes of a blind man and restored his sight. Jesus changed ordinary water into extraordinary wine. He took a lunch of ordinary fish and bread and from them made an extraordinary lunch for five thousand hungry people.

God does the unusual so that we recognize his unmistakable hand. I cannot take the credit for how things work out in my life. I cannot brag about my fine insights, good judgment, or special ability. God makes sure that his accomplishments are performed by him; it is his insight, his good judgment, and his ability that brings extraordinary results out of ordinary circumstances.

© MARILYN MEBERG

Have you noticed some peculiar quack-ups in Scripture? Things that behaved ... well ... rather oddly. For instance, Balaam's talking donkey. The only donkey I ever heard chatter was Frances the Talking Mule in the movies. No doubt Balaam, the rider, was startled when the donkey began to converse (Numbers 22). I've always thought it strange that the little boy's lunch box (John 6:9-14) turned into a cafeteria for thousands with leftovers. Now there's a lunch that smacks of entrepreneurial possibilities. Or what about the bowl of flour and the jar of oil belonging to the widow who housed Elijah (1 Kings 17:10-16)? No matter how much they used, the containers of flour and oil were not exhausted until the famine was over. It was a gift that kept on giving.

The wonder of it all is that the Lord can use everything for whatever purposes he chooses. Not to mention everyone. He chooses oddities and odd ducks for his divine purposes.

© PATSY CLAIRMONT

Promises About
Common Pots & Odd Ducks

*God, who said, "Let light shine out of darkness,"
made his light shine in our hearts to give us the light
of the knowledge of the glory of God in the face of
Christ. But we have this treasure in jars of clay to
show that this all-surpassing power is from God and
not from us.*

 2 Corinthians 4:6-7

*In a large house there are articles not only of gold
and silver, but also of wood and clay; some are for
noble purposes and some for ignoble. If a man
cleanses himself from the latter, he will be an
instrument for noble purposes, made holy, useful
to the Master and prepared to do any good work.*

 2 Timothy 2:20-21

*O LORD, you are our Father. We are the clay, you
are the potter; we are all the work of your hand.*

 Isaiah 64:8

Our Good Shepherd

Do you know what I'm tired of? I'm tired of looking for things. I spend a great deal of energy—mental and physical—looking for lost, misplaced, and hidden stuff. I find the hunt frustrating, even maddening, and frequently unnecessary.

Take my glasses. You might as well; someone does every time I set them down. Keys, purse, and vital papers elude me.

Here's what I think would help me and others prone to lostness—Velcro bodies. Think about it. Instead of laying down my glasses, I'd just press them on the outside of my upper arm. Then, when I needed them, I'd have them.

Gratefully we do have a Good Shepherd who will seek out the stray lambs and bring them back to the safety of the fold. He promises he will never leave us or forsake us. He is one who sticks closer than a brother (or Velcro).

© PATSY CLAIRMONT

$\mathcal{M}$ost of the time when I say grace before a meal I say with conviction, "The LORD is my Shepherd, I shall not be in want!" Not because it's a short verse, which lets me feed my face sooner than saying a prayer, but because I really mean it.

"I shall not be in want." Now, that reminds me that I desire certain things: new draperies, new carpeting, new furniture. These are luxuries, not necessities, because I already have these things. I just want different ones. Know what I mean? God promises to provide all our *needs* according to his riches in glory in Christ Jesus. I know he will do that. And he delights in often giving us what we want as well.

When I say, "The LORD is my Shepherd, I shall not be in want," it's more than just something to recite before eating. It's an affirmation that the Good Shepherd is watching over all the affairs of my life and is making sure I'm taken care of.

© THELMA WELLS

Promises About
Our Good Shepherd

Jesus said, "I am the good shepherd; I know my sheep and my sheep know me—just as the Father knows me and I know the Father—and I lay down my life for the sheep."

 John 10:14-15

The LORD is my shepherd, I shall not be in want.
   He makes me lie down in green pastures,
he leads me beside quiet waters,
   he restores my soul.
He guides me in paths of righteousness
   for his name's sake.
Even though I walk
   through the valley of the shadow of death,
I will fear no evil,
   for you are with me;
your rod and your staff,
   they comfort me....
You prepare a table before me
   in the presence of my enemies.
You anoint my head with oil;
   my cup overflows.
Surely goodness and love will follow me
   all the days of my life,
and I will dwell in the house of the LORD
   forever.

Psalm 23

A Laugh Lifestyle

Ken, Jeff, Beth and I were about a half block from home one afternoon when Ken simply pulled the car over to the curb, wordlessly opened his door, got out, and began walking in the direction of our home. I, too, got out of the car and began walking. Jeff, taking his cue, got out of the backseat and headed for home. Our puzzled seven-year-old, Beth, watched us walking toward home. She finally called out from the back window, "Don't you think I'm too young to drive?"

One evening as we were eating dinner, Ken, having scooped out his baked potato from its jacket, simply tossed it over his shoulder. Within minutes, Jeff tossed his empty potato skin over his shoulder. Beth looked at me and said, "They're being childish, huh, Mama?"

"They certainly are, Beth."

With a happy smile, she tossed her potato skin over her shoulder and proclaimed, "I'm supposed to be childish!"

These are wonderful memories I hold in my head as evidence of a somewhat zany but fun lifestyle we practiced in our home.

© MARILYN MEBERG

A laugh lifestyle is predicated upon our attitude toward the daily stuff of life. When those tasks seem too dull to endure, figure out a way to make them fun; get creative and entertain yourself. If the stuff of life for you right now is not dull and boring but instead painful and overwhelming, find something in the midst of the pain that makes you smile or giggle anyway. There's always something somewhere ... even if you have to just pretend to laugh until you really do!

You need that joy break, so take at least one every day. Hey, how about twirling and flourishing in your kitchen, grocery store, or office?

Dear Father, you provide our safety, our security, our eternal hope. Because of those loving assurances, enable us to see the joy, feel the joy, and even twirl with joy. Thank you that you are our reason for joy each day. Amen.

© BARBARA JOHNSON

Promises About a
Laugh Lifestyle

The good man brings good things out of the good stored up in his heart. ... For out of the overflow of his heart his mouth speaks.

 Luke 6:45

A cheerful look brings joy to the heart, and good news gives health to the bones.

 Proverbs 15:30

Shout for joy to the LORD, all the earth.

 Psalm 100:1

Satisfy us in the morning with your unfailing love, O LORD, that we may sing for joy and be glad all our days.

 Psalm 90:14

The Fun of Laughter

A group of women in their mid-seventies gather together each week for a Bible study. To one of their scheduled times of study, two of the women came feeling unusually intense arthritic pain, one had a headache that had been hanging on for days, one felt mildly depressed, and the other two said they felt basically indifferent about everything in life.

Out of desperation, these six decided it certainly couldn't hurt anything so they started the fake "heh-heh." It sounded so dumb in their ears that they did end up in genuine fits of hearty laughter.

To their amazement, the arthritic pain lessened, the headache became less intense, and the depression and indifference seemed to give way to a feeling of greater well-being. Now they begin each of their weekly sessions with prayer, self-induced laughter, and then Bible study. Needless to say, I was touched and pleased by this testimony of God's healing touch from laughter.

© MARILYN MEBERG

Give yourself a gift today: enjoy your own personality. God does. Here are some fun, sometimes foolish, always productive ways to put a smile on your face:

Prepare for surprises: life's most treasured moments come unannounced.

Start a journal if you don't already have one. Write down five things you are thankful for today.

Find something to laugh about today. If all else fails, go get a joke book from the library, call the funniest person you know, or read this: What do you get when you cross an insomniac, an agnostic, and a dyslexic? Answer: A person who lies awake at night trying to decide if there really is a doG.

Do something artsy. Dance to Mozart. Redecorate one wall. Paint a picture. Write a poem.

Smile at yourself in the mirror. Wink back.

Take a power nap.

Protect your enthusiasm from the negativity of others. Avoid toxic people today. If you run into one anyway, treat yourself to a double latte.

© BARBARA JOHNSON

Promises About the Fun of Laughter

A wife of noble character who can find? She is worth far more than rubies. ... She is clothed with strength and dignity; she can laugh at the days to come.

    🌿 Proverbs 31:10, 25

The Sovereign LORD says, "My servants will sing out of the joy of their hearts."

    🌿 Isaiah 65:14

Light is shed upon the righteous and joy on the upright in heart. Rejoice in the LORD, you who are righteous, and praise his holy name.

    🌿 Psalm 97:11-12

Praise God with the sounding of the trumpet, praise him with the harp and lyre, praise him with tambourine and dancing, praise him with the strings and flute, praise him with the clash of cymbals, praise him with resounding cymbals.

    🌿 Psalm 150:3-5

Go With God's Flow

Some people live with a low-grade anxiety tugging at their spirit all day long. They go to sleep with it, wake up with it, carry it around at home, in town, to church, and with friends. Here's a remedy: Take the present moment and find something to laugh at. People who laugh, last.

It is never too late to spend time on the important things. It is never too late to do what makes you happy. There is always time to look around and see something beautiful. The secret to using time well is no secret at all. It is summed up in the Alcoholics Anonymous slogan: *One day at a time.* This is not only the best we can do, but the careful design of a Creator who knows what our needs are and how to meet them. Some of us will need to adapt that slogan to: One minute at a time. That's okay. This minute is a gift. As someone said, that's why we call it the present.

© BARBARA JOHNSON

One of the most delightful weekends I had spent was nearing an end. Two teenage girls approached me while I was counting out my vitamins. "What are all those pills for?" one of them asked.

"Well," I explained, "these two are for beautiful eyes, that little one is for pearly, white teeth ..."

The other girl interrupted me with, "Haven't been taking them long, have you?"

What a comeback! The Pioneer Girl retreat had been filled with laughter and hilarity, as well as sweet communion and meaningful interaction. And, to think ... I almost missed it.

Marilyn had signed me up to join her in teaching Pioneer Girls at our church. I was not thrilled. I didn't want to do this. But, as is always the case, God knew what I could not have known: that I *needed* this experience. I can tell you from my own experience, the very thing we say no to just might be God's blessing in disguise. He wants to mature us; he wants to get us out of our comfort zone. What are you resisting?

© LUCI SWINDOLL

Promises About Going With God's Flow

"*I* know the plans I have for you," declares the LORD, "plans to prosper you and not to harm you, plans to give you hope and a future."

 Jeremiah 29:11

*Y*ou guide me with your counsel, O LORD, and afterward you will take me into glory.

 Psalm 73:24

*I*n his heart a man plans his course, but the LORD determines his steps.

 Proverbs 16:9

*J*esus said, "Whoever believes in me, as the Scripture has said, streams of living water will flow from within him."

 John 7:38

Remembering

I'm a hunter. My weapon is a camera, and I keep it loaded. I've snapped pictures of whales, wild animals in the bush, cat fights, foreign cities, autumn leaves, great horned owls, parties, weddings, children playing, lightning, snowfalls, family, friends, strangers. Why, I hardly go to the corner without my camera. What if I miss something? I couldn't stand it. Wherever I go, I'm in search of a memory.

Remembering is important to God. He encourages us to make memories. Scripture is replete with verses on remembering. We're encouraged to remember days of old, the wonders of God, the Sabbath, God's deeds and our struggles, our Creator, our youth, and that life is short. On and on the commands to remember go.

If you've not yet begun to create memories, start now. Load up your camera with film, fill that pen with ink, and capture the miracles and wonders that come your way. Surround yourself with whatever it takes to be reminded. God is faithful. Don't ever forget that.

© Luci Swindoll

Laugh and be merry, remember, better the world
    with a song,
Better the world with a blow in the teeth of a wrong.
Laugh for the time is brief, a thread the length
    of a span.
Laugh, and be proud to belong to the old proud
    pageant of man.

Laugh and be merry: remember the olden time,
God made Heaven and Earth,
    for joy He took in a rhyme,
Made them, and filled them full with the strong red
    wine of His mirth,
The splendid joy of the stars: the joy of the earth.

So we must laugh and drink from the deep blue cup
    of the sky,
Join the jubilant song of the great stars sweeping by,
Laugh, and battle, and work, and drink
    of the wine outpoured
In the dear green earth, the sign of the joy
    of the Lord.

© JOHN MASEFIELD

Promises About Remembering

I will remember the deeds of the LORD; yes, I will remember your miracles of long ago.
I will meditate on all your works and consider all your mighty deeds. Your ways, O God, are holy. What god is so great as our God?
You are the God who performs miracles; you display your power among the peoples.

 Psalm 77:11-14

*A*ll the ends of the earth will remember and turn to the LORD, and all the families of the nations will bow down before him, for dominion belongs to the LORD and he rules over the nations.

 Psalm 22:27-28

*O*n my bed I remember you, LORD; I think of you through the watches of the night. ...
My soul clings to you; your right hand upholds me.

 Psalm 63:6, 8

Real Self-worth

$\mathcal{I}$ was asked to sing one New Year's Eve at a banquet. Mom was staying with me, and we were discussing what she would wear. I'd actually only been to one New Year's Eve banquet before but had underdressed.

I tried to find just the right clothes for my mom. I bought a sequined jacket that would look lovely with a black evening skirt. Mom loved it. "I'd never have bought this myself," she said, "but it's fun!"

Barry and my mom arranged that I would meet them at the banquet. I watched in horror as the other ladies went into the dining area in conservative church dresses. Not a sequin in sight!

I went in to see if my mom had arrived yet. There she was in all her glory, looking like an aircraft landing light. But she has a great sense of humor, and Mom had a lovely evening anyway.

A quiet beauty that you can't buy in any mall graces a godly woman. To that kind of woman this child rises up and calls her blessed.

© SHEILA WALSH

$\mathcal{I}$ attended a gala occasion recently to which I wore a dressy pants outfit with stylish heels. I felt spiffy ... until I arrived at the event. I was the only woman with slacks on, and I felt awkward. After a considerable time I spotted another gal in slacks, and I wondered if she would want to sit with me. Soon several others arrived in similar attire, and I no longer felt the need to bond.

Aren't we funny? We work hard to be originals and then fear our originality has made us different. I enjoy being center stage unless it's under a critical spotlight.

None of us has a corner on blunders. We are not one of a kind when it comes to gumming up the works. But we are exclusive in our mix of personalities, backgrounds, relationships, callings, and life choices. This means we are both like and unlike others.

People who seem most at home with themselves are not rocked by their faux pas. They are able to move past their flub-ups without absorbing them into their sense of worth.

© PATSY CLAIRMONT

Promises About Real Self-worth

How great is the love the Father has lavished on us, that we should be called children of God! And that is what we are!

 1 John 3:1

Jesus said, "Are not two sparrows sold for a penny? Yet not one of them will fall to the ground apart from the will of your Father. And even the very hairs of your head are all numbered. So don't be afraid; you are worth more than many sparrows."

 Matthew 10:29-31

You have been given fullness in Christ, who is the head over every power and authority.

 Colossians 2:10

If we are children, then we are heirs—heirs of God and co-heirs with Christ, if indeed we share in his sufferings in order that we may also share in his glory.

 Romans 8:17

Looking for Laughter

My neighbor Bob was putzing around with a mechanical green frog that is supposed to croak when you get within two feet of it. Apparently, this frog was not performing properly and in exasperation Bob said, "This frog has truly croaked ... it won't make a sound."

Last night, I made my uncertain way in the dark to my front door. I'd forgotten to leave the porch light on. Not knowing that Bob had replaced the mechanically dead croaker with one that functioned, I entered the croak zone unawares. My presence set the frog into a frenzy of croaking which did not stop until I got inside. I giggled to myself as I realized I would never be able to sneak in and out of my own house as long as this vigilant green frog was on duty.

Giggles in life usually come from little things. If we train ourselves to see them and then giggle with them, we get a "perk." Giggle potential is everywhere; we just need to slow down long enough to see it.

© MARILYN MEBERG

$\mathcal{M}$arilyn liked the pantsuit I had on, but we both noticed a little spot on the front of the jacket. I said, "Drive me to the cleaners. I'll take this off in the car and go home in my underwear. You'll take it in for me, won't you?" As Marilyn headed for the cleaners, I hunkered down in my panties and bra.

When we got to the cleaners, Marilyn took my clothes, opened the door, and left it wide open. I scrambled to hide behind my purse, a box of Kleenex, and the steering wheel. When Marilyn got back in the car I choked on a half-hysterical giggle. "Marilyn ... how could you leave that door open?"

In mock innocence she said, "I left the door open? How careless of me." Even now, in the recesses of my mind, I can still hear Marilyn's cackling laughter as she sped away.

I dare you to do something today that will make you giggle!

© LUCI SWINDOLL

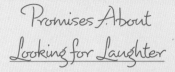

Promises About
Looking for Laughter

*Y*ou have made known to me the paths of life, O LORD; you will fill me with joy in your presence.

❧ Acts 2:28

*T*he joy of the LORD is your strength.

❧ Nehemiah 8:10

*T*he LORD is my strength and my shield; my heart trusts in him, and I am helped. My heart leaps for joy and I will give thanks to him in song.

❧ Psalm 28:7

*Y*ou make me glad by your deeds, O LORD; I sing for joy at the works of your hands.

❧ Psalm 92:4

A Joyful People

One day when my boys were little I came home from shopping and heard them in the kitchen shrieking with hilarity. They were flicking huge spoonfuls of raspberry Jell-O against a white wall at the far end of the kitchen and watching it ooze down to the floor.

I walked in and asked nonchalantly, "Where's my spoon?"

Tim promptly grabbed a soup ladle and handed it to me. I loaded it with a glob of goo and fired off. It hit the wall with a giant splat. Hey, this *was* fun! We laughed hysterically— even two hours later as they finished scrubbing the wall and floor.

Today, I wonder if my two oldest boys are laughing in heaven. I think about how the many hours of laughter we shared with Tim and Steve helped prepare us for their deaths. And when the losses of life became unbearable for me, I coped and learned to move on by cultivating a sense of humor. Humor turns everything around.

© BARBARA JOHNSON

Mrs. Davidson never appreciated my dad's easy laugh or his use of humor in the pulpit. If Dad said something she didn't agree with, she would shout out, "Pastor, that's a bunch of hooey!" He took it in stride and went on with his sermon.

One Sunday, Mrs. Davidson shouted, "Pastor, no one can laugh as much as you do and call himself a Christian."

Smiling, Dad spoke the rest of the hour about why joy needs to permeate every aspect of the Christian's life. Mrs. Davidson was unmoved. The congregation, however, clapped heartily when he concluded.

In the fourteenth century, my father would have been banned as well as cursed for his use of humor in the pulpit. But I'm heartened by the words of the twentieth-century C. S. Lewis, who wrote in *Reflections on the Psalms*, "A little comic relief in a discussion does no harm however serious the topic may be. In my own experience the funniest things have occurred in the gravest and most sincere conversations." My kind of man!

© MARILYN MEBERG

Promises About Joyful People

The LORD has done great things for us, and we are filled with joy.

 Psalm 126:3

Though you have not seen Christ, you love him; and even though you do not see him now, you believe in him and are filled with an inexpressible and glorious joy, for you are receiving the goal of your faith, the salvation of your souls.

 1 Peter 1:8-9

Joy is the echo of God's life within us.

 Joseph Marmion

Playtime Happiness

They say three kinds of people populate the world: Those who can count and those who can't. As you can see, I'm in the latter category. Despite my math deficiency, uncertainty, and puzzlement, there's one problem I don't have. I'm not like certain pious Christians who suffer from the haunting fear that someone, somewhere, may be happy.

We have to be on the lookout for fun, whether it be in simple things like funny signs ("Our fish are so fresh you want to smack 'em!"); funny names (if Fanny Brice had married Vic Tanny, her name would have been Fanny Tanny); or funny bumper stickers ("Forget about World Peace. Visualize using your turn signal.").

Find out what brings you joy. Have fun in a myriad of ways. Don't put it off until you finish your chores; instead, make tedious tasks a game. Compete with yourself. Reward yourself. Make work, play. Be curious about everything and everyone. You'll get tickled in the process!

© BARBARA JOHNSON

*L*uci is a sticker artisan. Using stickers, she creatively expresses herself in ways that make you giggle and bless your heart. When Luci invited me to join the group for a day of sticker investigating, the childlike part of my heart perked up.

I skipped my way to the racks, which beckoned like candy counters crowded with yummy choices. As I filled my bag, it began to overflow. No wonder we give children guidelines. The more I took the more I wanted. At one point during our rampage, our friend Judy collapsed on the floor in giggles, bedecked in sticker streamers. Finally, I mentally and physically dragged myself away from the enticing racks and headed for the van. On the two-and-a-half-hour trip back to the hotel, we all tried to organize our gazillion stickers while we giggled and chortled over our day. Whee!

How long has it been since you skipped? Slurped Popsicles? Hopscotched? Give yourself permission to take a break and celebrate. Then press on into childlike faith and enjoy the bounty of delights God has provided us.

© PATSY CLAIRMONT

Promises About Happiness

Is anyone happy? Let him sing songs of praise.

 James 5:13

To the man who pleases him, God gives wisdom, knowledge and happiness.

Ecclesiastes 2:26

May the righteous be glad and rejoice before God; may they be happy and joyful.

Psalm 68:3

The happiest heart that ever beat
Was in some quiet breast
That found the common daylight sweet,
And left to Heaven the rest.

John Vance Cheney

The Laugh Lines of Aging

I can remember the days when I bounded from bed in the morning, motor revving, ready to face the world. Today sludge moves faster than I do.

My body's soundtrack combines the creaks of an ancient door with the travailing of a birthing basset hound. My bed-head does add humor, doesn't yours? Hair skittering in all directions with occasional wads spewing up like oil wells and knotted clumps secured to the scalp.

Here's the good news. We can only get better looking now that we're up. A good brushing, curling, back combing, spraying, and our hair begins to make sense. Once we've adorned our frames with fashions, shod our feet with footwear, and covered our crevices with makeup, we are ready for a new day.

Actually, I need this rigorous morning regimen to thoroughly wake me up. It shakes out the kinks in my body, dislodges the corrosion from my brain cells, and reactivates my lethargic will. Even when our bones lack their original suppleness, may our wretched morning rumblings and grumblings turn to peals of praises.

© PATSY CLAIRMONT

Television journalist Dan Rather once asked a 106-year-old man to disclose his secret of long life. The old man rocked back and forth in his chair before answering. Finally he replied, "Keep breathing."

Sure, growing older is stressful, but using your funny bone to subdue that kind of stress works wonders! When you hear snap, crackle, pop, and it isn't your cereal, don't panic. Laughter defuses insults, soothes aching muscles, and counteracts the humiliation of what is happening to your body and mind.

Gerontologist Ann E. Gerike says we can develop a new way of thinking about our physical limitations as we age. After a lifetime of straining to be "the perfect perky ideal," finally your breasts can relax. And that extra weight around the middle (hence the term "middle age"?)—it's just cuddlier body lines! So as birthdays come, don't think of yourself as growing old; you've just reached that vibrant metallic age: silver in your hair, gold in your teeth, and lead in your bottom!

BARBARA JOHNSON

Promises About Aging

The unfading beauty of a gentle and quiet spirit ... is of great worth in God's sight.

 1 Peter 3:4

The righteous will flourish like a palm tree, they will grow like a cedar of Lebanon; planted in the house of the LORD, they will flourish in the courts of our God. They will still bear fruit in old age, they will stay fresh and green, proclaiming, "The LORD is upright; he is my Rock, and there is no wickedness in him."

 Psalm 92:12-15

Gray hair is a crown of splendor; it is attained by a righteous life.

 Proverbs 16:31

A Fallen Perspective

*I*n Japan a noodle museum is all the rage. Honest. It's far more popular than the art museums, which are generally visited only by scholars.

Imagine if someone could combine the two. The "Mona Lisa" could be done in rigatoni (be hard for her not to smirk). Or picture "Whistler's Mother" trying to rock on a chair of macaroni.

Actually, the noodle museum is dedicated to the ramen noodle, which is as popular in Japan as hot dogs are in Chicago's O'Hare Airport. In one year the Japanese wolf down enough noodles at the museum's nine ramen shops to encircle the globe five times. Wow! Imagine if it rained. It could give new meaning to wet noodle.

I think this news proves how off our noodles we humans are. We just can't keep things in balance. We are fallen people with strange ways. So, Lord, untie our noodley brains lest we become wise in our own eyes.

© PATSY CLAIRMONT

$\mathcal{I}$ was just about to leave for university. I needed a new look. So I bought a *Vogue* magazine and studied all the pictures. One model had hair that was softly permed. She looked beautiful. I took the picture to a small salon in my hometown and asked one of the stylists if she could do it.

I decided not to look until she was finished. I wanted a big surprise. I got one. My hair was layered different lengths on each side. I looked as if I'd stuck my finger in an electric socket.

I spotted my mom and my brother waiting for me. Stephen was laughing so hard he was clinging to a pole to hold himself up. My mother was attempting to make him behave, but her efforts caused him to laugh harder.

Thankfully I've learned that my worth to God has nothing to do with how I look or feel. If, as you look in the mirror, you wonder if this is a face only a mother could love, remember, it's a face a *Father* loves!

© SHEILA WALSH

Promises About Perspective

The LORD does not look at the things man looks at. Man looks at the outward appearance, but the LORD looks at the heart.

 1 Samuel 16:7

Oh, the depth of the riches of the wisdom and knowledge of God! How unsearchable his judgments, and his paths beyond tracing out!
"Who has known the mind of the Lord? Or who has been his counselor?"
"Who has ever given to God, that God should repay him?" For from him and through him and to him are all things. To him be the glory forever! Amen.

Romans 11:33-36

"Where then does wisdom come from? Where does understanding dwell? It is hidden from the eyes of every living thing, concealed even from the birds of the air. ... God understands the way to it and he alone knows where it dwells.

Job 28:20-21, 23

God's Strong Arm of Help

$\mathcal{I}$ remember the time I wound my foot around my neck (I was much younger) in an attempt to duplicate a trick by a TV contortionist. I managed to slide my foot around the back of my neck, but when my toes hooked close to my ear, I couldn't unwind myself. It took just seconds to realize what an unnatural position this was so I yelled to my husband for help.

Les was amazed when he tromped into the room and saw his wife in a virtual knot. He dislodged my foot, releasing the pressure off my cramping leg. I appreciated his assistance but was a tad irritated at his incessant snickering during the unwinding process.

Our own silly fascinations remind us that sometimes we let life get out of whack. Just check what's out of place in your life. It could be interests that become fetishes, or some less-than-bright action you've taken. Fortunately, even if we fall on our behind, God's everlasting arms pick us up, and he embraces us with his loving-kindness.

© PATSY CLAIRMONT

"Honey, you have to get out the door for school."

I popped into my eight-year-old's room, surprised to find him lying on his bed, hands behind his head, staring at the ceiling.

"Sweetheart, what are you doing?"

"I'm thinking it's too late for my mind and too late for my body."

Biting my lower lip to prevent a giggle, I asked him how long he thought his mind and body would be in that state.

"Maybe all day."

I let him stay home. And Jeff never complained again about his mind and body feeling too late, but went off to school the next day on schedule.

God has created within all human beings a tremendous drive to survive, [yet] most of us have barely tapped into our potential. Do you suppose a few of us are lying on our beds with our hands behind our head, thinking, *It's too late for my mind and too late for my body?* May I be settled into the truth that I can do all things through Christ who strengthens me.

MARILYN MEBERG

Promises About God's Strength

I can do everything through Christ who gives me strength.

 Philippians 4:13

The eternal God is your refuge, and underneath are the everlasting arms.

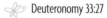 Deuteronomy 33:27

To him who is able to keep you from falling and to present you before his glorious presence without fault and with great joy—to the only God our Savior be glory, majesty, power and authority, through Jesus Christ our Lord, before all ages, now and forevermore! Amen.

 Jude 24-25

The LORD gives strength to his people.

 Psalm 29:11

Oops!

 received a statement from my checking account, advising that a charge had been levied. I simply couldn't understand why. Well, I thought, I'll just go to Fidelity Federal and set things straight.

The next day I parked in front of the bank, grabbed the statement, flounced inside, marched right up to the teller, and pontificated, "I got this statement in the mail informing me of a charge of $11.88, but I've never even used this account. I'd like you to waive this service charge, please, right now."

When I finished blasting out my request the woman behind the counter finally said, "I'd like to, lady, but this is Wells Fargo Bank."

The village idiot, crawling out the bank's side door, heard the tellers whispering: "Can you believe that woman ... she doesn't even have an account in this bank?"

I got in my car and laughed my head off. We've got to be able to laugh at our own mistakes. None of us is infallible. We make mistakes in life, and more often than not, they're funny.

© LUCI SWINDOLL

$\mathcal{I}$ had been invited to take a horseback ride. Kay, my lovely hostess, greeted me with enthusiasm. My husband's cautions rang in my ears as I surveyed the saddled horses.

Kay pointed to a horse and said Cecil would be my steed. I boarded my waiting transportation via a booster box. The only challenge I had was my stirrups. They were a little too long for my short legs, and I felt like a toe dancer as I stretched to keep my feet in the stirrups.

About six minutes into the ride, my back began whining. Evidently my aerobic lifestyle of bench-pressing the newspaper and hoisting the mail had not prepared me for this equine workout.

Finally, with a kink in my back the size of New Hampshire, the staff compassionately headed for the stable. For three days afterwards my back felt like Cecil had ridden me.

Do you find it difficult to take good advice? To live within your limitations? To admit when you're wrong? Just remember, if you get a backache from carrying your horse, don't be surprised.

© PATSY CLAIRMONT

Promises About
Making Mistakes

If we confess our sins, he is faithful and just and will forgive us our sins and purify us from all unrighteousness.

    1 John 1:9

Praise the LORD, O my soul, and forget not all his benefits—who forgives all your sins and heals all your diseases, who redeems your life from the pit and crowns you with love and compassion, who satisfies your desires with good things so that your youth is renewed like the eagle's.

    Psalm 103:2-5

"I will repay you for the years the locusts have eaten," says the LORD.

    Joel 2:25

Finding Eternal Good Humor

*L*ike many women, I have bags of costume jewelry. The faux jewelry is counterfeit. It looks pretty for a while, but then it begins to fade, peel, and break. If you wear it in water long enough, it will turn your skin green.

Genuine versus counterfeit. Real versus fake. Joy versus happiness. Joy gives me calm assurance even though I go through the valley of the shadow of death. Joy enables me to hold my peace when people say and do ugly things to me. When we go through troubles, afflictions, persecution, danger, illness, and distress, when the enemy comes to steal, kill, and destroy, we can have genuine joy in our hearts.

Joy is permanent. Once you have it, you never lose it. It may be overshadowed by human frailties, but real joy lasts for eternity.

© THELMA WELLS

Human beings thrive on laughter. Since most of us can't afford vacations in Hawaii, we have to learn to make our own fun! The best way to do that is to keep your state of mind green and golden: find, recycle, or produce joy wherever and however you can. A good humorist is a work of heart! The Hasidic Jews believe that the best way to worship God is by being happy. They even incorporate dance and celebration into their spiritual walk.

Humor is the chocolate chips in the ice cream of life. Remember the old-time "Good Humor Man" who drove his ice cream truck down every street in the neighborhood, chiming a jingle on those hot summer days? All the kids came running as soon as they heard the sound. But good humor doesn't drive down many streets anymore. You have to go out and get it yourself.

Fortunately, it's not that hard to find.

© BARBARA JOHNSON

Promises About Finding Eternal Good Humor

Jesus said, "Now is your time of grief, but I will see you again and you will rejoice, and no one will take away your joy."

 John 16:22

Those who sow in tears will reap with songs of joy. He who goes out weeping, carrying seed to sow, will return with songs of joy, carrying sheaves with him.

 Psalm 126:5-6

Give thanks to the LORD, for he is good; his love endures forever.

 Psalm 118:1

Free at Last

Being a clown-like gal with my impish ways, I could be a little partial, but it's more than clowns' comical attire, their water-filled flowers, or their bulbous horns that endear them to the world. I think the big appeal is their outrageous freedom to play the fool, the mime, the juggler, the victim, the hero, the Keystone cop, or the lost waif. Yes, a clown can be whomever she chooses, not only without opposition but also to rousing applause.

While we tend to give circus clowns encores for their expressive freedom, we generally are not as generous with each other. In fact, it's not easy to be oneself without running into opposition. Rules, expectations, belief systems, and opinions can keep us mired in legalism and criticism. The good news is that Jesus came for clowns like us, to set us free from the clowns who would cast buckets full of stones in our direction. And stones are something Jesus was acquainted with. The Pharisees' knotted beliefs kept them so bound to the law that they missed love and the Liberator.

© Patsy Clairmont

Because of an unexpected delay in a return flight from Dallas, I wandered into an airport bookstore with the intention of picking up a pleasant "no-brainer" since I had finished reading everything I'd brought with me.

Hours later, as we lurched onto the windswept runway in Palm Springs, I finished the book and smiled happily. "Marilyn," I said to myself, "when was the last time you settled in for a mindlessly pleasant read? Why don't you do that more often?"

With an abruptness that matched the plane's grinding halt, it hit me that I had settled into some legalistic thinking about my reading habits. Unless my reading contributed to my spiritual or intellectual growth, I didn't take the time. Not to allow myself any other kind of reading was unbalanced and a bit narrow.

Wouldn't it be fun occasionally to produce nothing, accomplish nothing, and contribute to nothing? Maybe that means reading a book that doesn't require a pen, or meander through the mall or stroll (not jog) through the park. The possibilities for nothing are endless.

© MARILYN MEBERG

Promises About Freedom

_If_ the Son sets you free, you will be free indeed.

🌸 John 8:36

_W_here the Spirit of the Lord is, there is freedom.

🌸 2 Corinthians 3:17

_I_ run in the path of your commands, LORD, for you have set my heart free.

🌸 Psalm 119:32

_It_ is for freedom that Christ has set us free.

🌸 Galatians 5:1

_Y_ou will know the truth, and the truth will set you free.

🌸 John 8:32

Peculiar People

$\mathcal{S}$ome ladies come to the Women of Faith conferences headed in the opposite direction from the rest of the world. That's the impression TJ gave at a conference attended by fifteen thousand women. While other women were applauding, TJ waved a white, size 44D, lace brassiere in the air, and yelled "Hallelujah." All her parish pals could do was act as if they didn't know her.

She ran up to my book table during a break with the bra in hand and insisted, "Please sign my bra! Sign it right here!"

I thought, *If TJ has the nerve to sling a bra around and then ask me to autograph it, that's the least I can do.* I signed it, "My cup runneth over!"

I saw it all as great fun. And I learned that not all people who act a little over-the-top should be labeled "off sides" just because they do things differently from the norm. You really can't judge a book by its cover. You have to look inside to see how the pages read.

© THELMA WELLS

As I travel across the country to various speaking engagements, I meet concealed hurt, disguised hurt, disjointed hurt. Pain is a normal part of life.

That's why I think: Why not take as much joy as possible along the way so when hurt comes, we assimilate it better?

Every day now I take joy—by refusing to accept the lie that I have to feel miserable about the baggage, the stuff, and the sickness that trails me no matter how I try to hide or outwit it. I choose to do zany, kooky, and funny things to make myself and others laugh.

And I fling joy—beyond my next-door neighbor's fence, clear across town, and into the universe. Then it curves right back to me. Sometimes with a whack on the head when I need it. Sometimes with a thwack into my heart. Sometimes landing with a crack at my feet. But it always comes back. No doubt about it.

© BARBARA JOHNSON

Promises About Peculiar People

You are a people holy to the LORD your God.

 Deuteronomy 14:2

The LORD has declared this day that you are his people, his treasured possession as he promised, and that you are to keep all his commands. He has declared that he will set you in praise, fame and honor high above all the nations he has made and that you will be a people holy to the LORD your God, as he promised.

 Deuteronomy 26:18-19

Jesus Christ ... gave himself for us to redeem us from all wickedness and to purify for himself a people that are his very own, eager to do what is good.

 Titus 2:13-14

You are a chosen people, a royal priesthood, a holy nation, a people belonging to God, that you may declare the praises of him who called you out of darkness into his wonderful light.

 1 Peter 2:9

Tombstone Thoughts

A few short words sometimes capture the entire essence of a person. It is my understanding that W. C. Fields, for example, has etched on his tombstone, "On the whole, I'd rather be here than in Philadelphia." And how about the woman who had her potato salad recipe carved into her headstone. Apparently, during her lifetime everybody wanted that recipe and her response was always: "Over my dead body." I have a close friend who never gets quite as much sympathy as she likes when she's feeling bad, so she wants to be remembered by these loving words: "See, I told you I was sick."

Most of us won't have the prerogative to write our own epitaph. It will be written by someone else ... someone who will seek to capture a single phrase epitomizing our entire life. For some of us, the message on our tombstone seems like something in the far-distant future. However, we never know. If you were to die today, what phrase captures your essence? What words characterize you?

© LUCI SWINDOLL

Sally is visiting Mary. She talks of the adventures she has had and continues to have in God. There were failures and bruises and dark moments, but there was life every step of the way.

Mary smiles a little, and pours more tea. "You always were the one for adventures, Sally!" she says with a shake of her head.

"Yes," Sally replies, the creases around her eyes deepening as she smiles. "Life is good. God is good! Well, I must be off. Take good care of yourself, Mary." She reaches over to hug her friend goodbye.

"I will," Mary says wistfully as Sally heads down the path. "I always have."

Which woman do you want to be like? The one who played it safe and has no runs in her hose, or the one who threw herself in, who threw open the windows to God and to the world and was covered in sunshine in the process? Start where you are and just do it! Make little waves of your own, and God will put the wind into your sails.

© SHEILA WALSH

Promises About
Your Life's Direction

Trust in the LORD with all your heart and lean not on your own understanding; in all your ways acknowledge him, and he will make your paths straight.

❧ Proverbs 3:5-6

This is what the LORD says-your Redeemer, the Holy One of Israel: "I am the LORD your God, who teaches you what is best for you, who directs you in the way you should go."

❧ Isaiah 48:17

God is our God for ever and ever; he will be our guide even to the end.

❧ Psalm 48:14

Whether you turn to the right or to the left, your ears will hear a voice behind you, saying, "This is the way; walk in it."

❧ Isaiah 30:21

Laughter
IS
GOOD MEDICINE

Never Give Up Hope

Hope is a precious gift of our salvation. While we can "hope" that our kids don't spill their soda, we must remember that our only reliable hope is in what we cannot see or control: the outrageous faithfulness of God. Our responsibility to him as his children is to study his character so we will know, without a doubt, that whatever way he deals with our circumstances in life, it's the right way. Even when things don't work out the way we planned or desired, he is all-knowing, all-loving, the beginning and the ending. Hope is acting on the conviction that despite what we see with the natural eye, God is working in the spiritual realm to accomplish his perfect will in our lives. His hope does not disappoint!

God's Word declares hope. God's promises proclaim hope. We must think hope. Speak hope. Pray hope. Sing hope. Act hope. Share hope. In other words, get our hopes up. Because hope has been given to us, we can expect the best, even in the worst conditions. Praise God!

© Sheila Walsh

One of the most colorful people in my family is Lawrence Morris, Jr., my mother's only brother. His nickname is Uncle Brother. At more than seventy years old, he tries to act and think like a springtime chicken.

Although he had accepted Christ as a young man, Uncle Brother lived like the devil. He had his share of booze and all that goes with it. But even when I was angry with him for the way he treated everyone, he knew I loved him.

Thanks be to God, Uncle Brother has made some major changes. Now he praises God. He reads his Bible. He bridles his tongue. He speaks affectionately about people. He has changed his friends. He is respected in his community. He is concerned about family members. He attends family celebrations. He's fun to be around.

Are you dealing with someone whom you feel will never change? Nobody is so far from God that he can't get back to the Lord. Thank God for what he will do. Patiently but expectantly wait on the Lord. Renew your hope!

THELMA WELLS

Promises About Hope

Hope deferred makes the heart sick, but a longing fulfilled is a tree of life.

 Proverbs 13:12

Why are you downcast, O my soul? Why so disturbed within me? Put your hope in God, for I will yet praise him, my Savior and my God.

 Psalm 42:11

Everything that was written in the past was written to teach us, so that through endurance and the encouragement of the Scriptures we might have hope.

Romans 15:4

The word which God has written on the brow of every man is Hope.

 Victor Hugo

Finding Peace

The accent may be on youth these days, but the stress is on adults. Always reflecting on the things we haven't done, we start each day worrying earlier and stay up later to worry every night.

A certain parish priest patented a method for making holy water. I figure it's a good way to deal with worries, too. He took a big pot, filled it with water, turned up the heat, and boiled the devil out of it.

And guilt? Why not boil the devil out of that, too? After all, we'll always have those things we shouldn't have done but did anyway. So we end up wasting time dragging our burden of guilt in the dirt instead of getting it washed.

Cares are the tools God uses to fashion us for better things. He uses reverses to move us forward. Reverses and cares bow us down low until we finally drop to our knees. But a lot of kneeling keeps us in good standing because it brings us closer to God. Being close to God, we find peace.

© BARBARA JOHNSON

We don't see a lot of cannons around anymore—except in cartoons that depict people being shot out of them and laughing all the way. Whoever came up with that idea anyway? A cannon was a deadly weapon of war. Big, heavy, wrought iron, with an imposing barrel, breech, and firing mechanism that propelled seven-hundred-pound balls that demolished anything or anybody within range.

Sometimes life's heartaches and disappointments look like cannonballs—heading straight toward us. And baby, it ain't funny when you're shot out of the cannon in real life, either. Every week I talk with people who are battling the heavy artillery of life. Depression, oppression, loneliness, barrenness. Seven hundred pounds is a light load for some of these women because they already feel like the weight of the world is on their shoulders.

But we have a shield: the Spirit of God. The ammunition of abuse doesn't have to penetrate our souls. In the midst of the battle, we can experience a "peace that passes understanding." That peace is available to all who trust God.

© THELMA WELLS

Promises About Peace

Jesus said, "Peace I leave with you; my peace I give you. I do not give to you as the world gives. Do not let your hearts be troubled and do not be afraid."

 John 14:27

The LORD blesses his people with peace.

 Psalm 29:11

You, LORD, will keep in perfect peace him whose mind is steadfast, because he trusts in you.

 Isaiah 26:3

The fruit of righteousness will be peace; the effect of righteousness will be quietness and confidence forever.

Isaiah 32:17

Worthless Worrying

"How long have you had this germ thing?" Luci asked after questioning why I was eating my entire cafeteria meal with an over-sized spoon I had found in an obscure container hidden behind the soft ice-cream machine.

"Since the sixth grade science teacher had us all touch some specially treated sponge, and overnight it grew bacteria cultures that we watched develop into various colorful and horrifying configurations. I've never been the same since."

Luci slowly put down her fork and studied it for a second. Then, with renewed enthusiasm, she announced, "If those germs haven't gotten me by this time in my life, I don't think they ever will!"

Her healthy response reminded me that for me to fear the unseen and worry about its potential to do harm throttles my joy. God has created within each of us a miraculously effective immune system.

Keep everything in perspective. Rest in God's provision.

MARILYN MEBERG

Do you experience times when there doesn't seem to be enough to go around? Bills are piling up faster than paychecks, and anxiety is creeping into your mind.

Many such moments have occurred for me, making me acutely aware that the bread on my plate came from the Lord because my cupboard was bare. When I was part of British Youth for Christ, I was paid a minimal salary. Usually I had just enough to keep me in hose and shampoo—and on my knees.

When you find yourself looking at a bank balance that couldn't keep a goldfish afloat, remember whose you are. God knows every unexpected turn of events. We are told by Paul to be anxious about nothing. "Nothing" is a pretty conclusive word. No thing, no part, no portion.

Whatever is weighing you down, stop what you're doing (which I guess at the moment is reading!), and with thanksgiving on your lips, bring your requests to God.

© SHEILA WALSH

Promises About Worry

Cast your cares on the LORD and he will sustain you; he will never let the righteous fall.

 Psalm 55:22

Jesus said to his disciples, "Do not worry about your life, what you will eat; or about your body, what you will wear. Life is more than food, and the body more than clothes. Consider the ravens: They do not sow or reap, they have no storeroom or barn; yet God feeds them. And how much more valuable you are than birds!"

 Luke 12:22-24

Do not be anxious about anything, but in every-thing, by prayer and petition, with thanksgiving, present your requests to God. And the peace of God, which transcends all understanding, will guard your hearts and your minds in Christ Jesus.

 Philippians 4:6-7

Busy Day Boosters

Sometimes at the end of a busy day, when I think about all the things I never got around to, I try to look at things differently: upside down, inside out, or with light shining on the dark side.

Kids love the way light shines through crystal, ricochets off diamonds, emanates from rainbows. Crystals, diamonds, and rainbows are all designed by God. He put them in the world to remind us to take things lightly. He means for us to wonder what could be hidden in the darkest piece of coal or the rainiest day on earth. Kids never think they have all the answers, and we shouldn't either. Thinking we know it all closes our hearts to what is beautiful and new.

Next time you're walking in the dark and feel like you haven't laughed for a long, long time, try standing on your head. Look at your world in a way you've never done before. I guarantee it'll make a kid of you, just the right kind of kid for God's kingdom.

BARBARA JOHNSON

I feel encased within a timepiece that can at times rob me of my peace. Left unto ourselves, some of us would race and others of us would rust. Either way we would speed past or sleep through the joy. We need to make peace with the timepiece so we don't spend our time beating our heads against the clock.

Here are some tips. I'll try them if you will.

1. Don't cram everyday so full you can't enjoy the journey.

2. Don't under-plan and miss the thrill of a fruitful day.

3. Don't underestimate a nap, a rocking chair, and a good book.

4. Don't become a sloth.

5. Do offer your gratitude for the moments assigned to you.

6. Do celebrate even the passing of days.

© PATSY CLAIRMONT

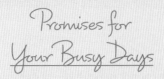

Promises for Your Busy Days

This is what the LORD Almighty, the God of Israel, says ..."I will refresh the weary and satisfy the faint."

 Jeremiah 31:23, 25

God gives strength to the weary and increases the power of the weak.
Even youths grow tired and weary, and young men stumble and fall; but those who hope in the LORD will renew their strength. They will soar on wings like eagles; they will run and not grow weary, they will walk and not be faint.

 Isaiah 40:29-31

He who dwells in the shelter of the Most High will rest in the shadow of the Almighty.

Psalm 91:1

A Right Response

I cannot prevent the perplexities of life, but I can choose how I respond to them. When I need a pity party, I literally set my clock for fifteen minutes. Within that time frame, I whine and wail, beat myself up, throw a temper tantrum, break something, or whatever I feel is appropriate to my circumstances at the moment. When the alarm sounds, I know that's my cue to cut it out.

Admittedly, sometimes I've had to set the clock four times before I got it all out of my system! But I think that one hour is long enough to stay in a state of insanity. After I've used up my four times to reset the clock, I force myself to STOP. I force myself to start praise music. I force myself to pray. I just say, "Jesus, Jesus, Jesus." The enemy of our soul flees at the name of Jesus.

While in this process, I calm down. I start thinking more clearly. I'm not as inclined to make irrational decisions. If this works for me, it will certainly work for you.

© THELMA WELLS

"Did you mail that insurance form, sweetie?" I asked Barry one afternoon.

He seemed to lose a little color. "I forgot," he said.

"Why would you forget something as important as that?" I snapped.

"I'm sorry, honey. I just forgot," he said.

I found myself standing on the edge of a cliff and knew I had to choose whether I would dive off or back off. I asked Barry to excuse me for a moment, and I made a conscious, determined choice to get on my knees and to let my anger go. As I released my fury, I was filled with joy.

Choosing to let go of my tempestuous responses may not seem big to you, but it's making a huge difference in our lives. I want to be the fragrance of Christ in the midst of the storms of life, not part of the storm front.

If you struggle with old behaviors that are as familiar to you as the spider veins on your legs, I encourage you to invite Christ into the moment and to let those old patterns go. You can choose. You can be a drip of rain or a ray of sunshine.

SHEILA WALSH

Promises About Our Response to Trouble

We know that in all things God works for the good of those who love him, who have been called according to his purpose.

 Romans 8:28

For Christ's sake, I delight in weaknesses, in insults, in hardships, in persecutions, in difficulties. For when I am weak, then I am strong.

 2 Corinthians 12:10

Our present sufferings are not worth comparing with the glory that will be revealed in us.

 Romans 8:18

Blessed is the man who perseveres under trial, because when he has stood the test, he will receive the crown of life that God has promised to those who love him.

 James 1:12

An Attitude of Praise

Praising God in song lifts our spirits, clears our heads, and opens a place for the Holy Spirit to speak to us.

Alaya, my one-and-a-half-year-old granddaughter, is always singing—when she is eating, having her diaper changed, playing, standing, pulling up, watching television, bouncing in her swing, sitting in a car, attending church. Everywhere, all the time, she has a song in her heart.

Alaya has loving parents whom she can depend on to take care of her, comfortable and safe surroundings to live in, little responsibility, a love of singing, lots of attention when she sings, and joy because in her little heart she feels God's love.

Just as Alaya feels secure and loved, God offers the same to his children. He extends care to us by meeting our every need and comforting us when we go through trials.

Don't you think we have something to sing about? Want to lift your spirits from the hustle and bustle of the day? Sing to the Lord. When praises go up, blessings come down. Now, isn't that something to sing about?

© THELMA WELLS

$\mathscr{I}$'ll never forget Joanne DeGraw. She died of cancer, which she battled bravely for seventeen years.

Joanne had a great sense of humor in spite of the severity of her physical condition. Whether we were discussing the latest book we had read, an opera we had seen together, the Scriptures, her children, or my home-decorating project, she injected her flair for the funny in her sweet Southern twang.

We spent long days in front of a roaring fire, talking and laughing, reading aloud, eating, cooking, and chatting about dreams, joys, and regrets. The seriousness of her diagnosis didn't set the tone for our day; her indomitable spirit did.

Joanne could have made her suffering a time of emotional torment for herself and anguish for her loved ones, but she didn't. She decided instead to accept the path God gave her with courage, grace, and humor. Without denying her reality, she chose to think on what was excellent and praiseworthy.

LUCI SWINDOLL

Promises About Praise

I will praise you as long as I live, LORD, and in your name I will lift up my hands. My soul will be satisfied as with the richest of foods; with singing lips my mouth will praise you.

 Psalm 63:4-5

*P*raise be to the God and Father of our LORD Jesus Christ, who has blessed us in the heavenly realms with every spiritual blessing in Christ. For he chose us in him before the creation of the world to be holy and blameless in his sight.

Ephesians 1:3-4

*A*s the soil makes the sprout come up and a garden causes seeds to grow, so the Sovereign LORD will make righteousness and praise spring up before all nations.

Isaiah 61:11

Surviving Struggles

*L*et your joy out. One way I do that is to give people something to laugh about. How? I collect jokes and write down everything I hear that makes me brighten up. I make amusement a ministry because chuckles are better than a therapist. They are aloe vera for the sunburns of life. When the dumps take their toll, laughter provides the exact change to get you through.

Whatever your troubles, try looking at them by the light of another source or a different star. Go ahead; don't be afraid. Find a wacky angle, a new twist. Offer trouble a little serious thought, then turn it upside down and look at it through God-colored glasses. Chew on trouble's possibilities for making you smarter, better, stronger, kinder. Sample some weird and wonderful Jelly Bellies, Gobstoppers, or Sweet Tarts while you do that. Then take the curved weapon I call joy and toss trouble by its funny side out into the world.

© BARBARA JOHNSON

How do we enjoy God's grace in the midst of tough times? First we have to make a habit of drinking deeply of the grace God promises, every moment. We have to uncover our soul and let grace soak us to our roots.

Second, we have to keep our sense of humor. I find it helpful to have a few things up my sleeve for those tougher-than-usual days when the melons are landing on my head. I have several funny videos that just knock me over. Photographs of my friends and family always cheer me up. So does getting out into the fresh air and walking across the field to watch my neighbor's horses. Christian and I lie on our backs on the grass and wait for the moon to come out. Sometimes I read one of my favorite Psalms.

God is all around us, longing to talk to us, to love us, to lift us up. Make up your own survival kit. Find things that you know can lift you above the hubbub in your house and in your head.

SHEILA WALSH

Promises About Struggles

When the storm has swept by, the wicked are gone, but the righteous stand firm forever.

🌸 Proverbs 10:25

Just as the sufferings of Christ flow over into our lives, so also through Christ our comfort overflows.

🌸 2 Corinthians 1:5

God knows the way that I take; when he has tested me, I will come forth as gold.

🌸 Job 23:10

Consider it pure joy ... whenever you face trials of many kinds, because you know that the testing of your faith develops perseverance.

🌸 James 1:2-3

We also rejoice in our sufferings, because we know that suffering produces perseverance; perseverance, character; and character, hope. And hope does not disappoint us, because God has poured out his love into our hearts by the Holy Spirit, whom he has given us.

🌸 Romans 5:3-5

Turn the Tables on Trouble

✿

A crazy character on a PBS sitcom just cracks me up. She is ridiculously pretentious and surrounded by a cast of hilarious friends and family members. Her long-suffering husband has been "gifted" with early retirement and now has days full of time with his silly wife. The vicar of her church runs every time he sees her coming, and the neighbor always spills her coffee on the carpet because this crazy lady makes her nervous.

Every now and then Barry and I will grab a bag of chips and salsa. I'll make some hot tea and haul a sack of chocolate chip cookies over to the television set. We'll stick in a tape and laugh.

It's good to let go and laugh when life is weighing you down. It won't change any of the circumstances you find yourself in, but when you can laugh at the antics of others, it helps to lighten the load.

© Sheila Walsh

Some say truth is stranger than fiction; others say it isn't stranger, just more rare. (One thing is sure: if you tell the truth, there's less to remember!)

No matter what, don't ever let yesterday use up too much of today. If it sneaks up on you, turn the tables on it. Like interest rates, make trouble work for you, not against you. You don't always need a comedian to make you laugh. Once you get started, you can pull a few one-liners out of the bag yourself. When someone says, "Life is hard," say, "I prefer it to the alternative, don't you?" When somebody else complains about getting old, answer, "Right now, I'm just sitting here being thankful that wrinkles don't hurt!"

Life is too short to spend it being angry, bored, or dull. That was never God's intention. Maybe boredom and dullness aren't on any list of sins in the Bible, but they will sap your joy if you tolerate them.

BARBARA JOHNSON

Promises About Turning the Tables on Trouble

Jesus said, "In this world you will have trouble. But take heart! I have overcome the world."

 John 16:33

I am greatly encouraged; in all our troubles my joy knows no bounds.

 2 Corinthians 7:4

I am convinced that neither death nor life, neither angels nor demons, neither the present nor the future, nor any powers, neither height nor depth, nor anything else in all creation, will be able to separate us from the love of God that is in Christ Jesus our Lord.

 Romans 8:38-39

The LORD is a refuge for the oppressed, a stronghold in times of trouble.

 Psalm 9:9

Happy Heartbeats

We live out the kingdom of God within us when we treasure each other and when we find ways to turn unfortunate things around. Laughter is one of those ways. Laughter stirs the blood, expands the chest, electrifies the nerves, and clears the cobwebs from the brain. If you laugh a lot, when you are older all your wrinkles will be in the right places!

If you live to be one hundred, your heart will have beat 3,681,619,200 times, pumping 27,323,260 gallons of blood weighing over one hundred tons. (If you end up tired, you've earned it!) Think about making every heartbeat a happy one.

BARBARA JOHNSON

$\mathcal{M}$y husband, Barry, and I have a list of activities for when the walls close in on us, when it's been a tough week, or when it has rained for the last ten days. We turn to a few friends on videotape and laugh till our cheeks ache.

Does something come to mind for you? It could be an old black-and-white episode of Andy Griffith or the time Lucy and Ethel worked in the chocolate factory. It might be a video of family and friends that makes you laugh when you watch it. Or maybe it's an old tearjerker movie with a happy ending. Pop in the tape, stock up on the snacks, and put your feet up. There's nothing like a vat of praline pecan ice cream and a good video when the bills are due, the laundry is piled to the ceiling, and the cat just coughed up a fur ball on the dog!

© SHEILA WALSH

Promises About a Happy Heart

You have made known to me the path of life,
O LORD; you will fill me with joy in your presence,
with eternal pleasures at your right hand.

 Psalm 16:11

Be glad ... rejoice in the LORD your God, for he has
given you the autumn rains in righteousness.
He sends you abundant showers, both autumn and
spring rains, as before.

 Joel 2:23

Weeping may remain for a night, but rejoicing
comes in the morning.

 Psalm 30:5

You turned my wailing into dancing; you removed
my sackcloth and clothed me with joy, that my heart
may sing to you and not be silent. O LORD my God, I
will give you thanks forever.

 Psalm 30:11-12

The Power of Faith

$\mathcal{E}$verybody experiences difficult situations in life. Things that make us want to scream out or give up. Deprivations. Sacrifices. Losses. Misunderstandings. But isn't there some way for the Christian to respond without getting mad at God? Otherwise, what's the good of our faith? There has to be some key to being joyful in the midst of discouraging circumstances and crabby people. What is it?

It's taking God at his Word. It's believing he will do what he says, no matter how things look or how we feel. Nobody said it would be easy. If you find any Scripture that even hints that life will be easy, call me collect. Please. But I can tell you now ... it ain't in there! However, trusting God with everything we have, everything we are, every problem that is ours, every loss we endure, every battle we face, every person who disappoints us—with thanksgiving— gives us the grace to come through it with flying colors.

LUCI SWINDOLL

Have you noticed that we are laughter and tears, dirges and dances, jubilations and consternations, hallelujahs and woes? We have good days, great days, and way-down-deep-in-the-pit days. Some seasons are easier than others, while some are downright impossible. For each of us, our days are unpredictable, and we tip the scales from preposterous to precious. Life is a gift bulging with mystery, intrigue, comedy, tragedy—and purpose.

When we realize our days here matter, our pain has significance, and our choices are meaningful, we can step through the darkest of times with hope in our hearts. It's not that we won't waver, but even our inquiries have the potential, when we are seeking, to lead us to a stronger faith.

I find that my joy is enlarged by understanding that, as a child of God, even my pain has purpose. That realization doesn't eliminate my pain, but it makes it more manageable, allowing me other emotions in the midst of calamity, including shocking pink joy.

PATSY CLAIRMONT

Promises About Faith

Jesus said, "I tell you the truth, if you have faith as small as a mustard seed, you can say to this mountain, 'Move from here to there' and it will move. Nothing will be impossible for you."

 Matthew 17:20

The prayer offered in faith will make the sick person well; the Lord will raise him up. If he has sinned, he will be forgiven.

Je James 5:15

In Christ and through faith in him we may approach God with freedom and confidence.

Je Ephesians 3:12

Righteousness from God comes through faith in Jesus Christ to all who believe.

Je Romans 3:22

The Star of the Show

I need to be reminded of who takes care of me and who is in charge of all the events in my life. When I'm congratulating myself on my confidence and skill, it's easy to forget who my safety net is. Fortunately, God doesn't let me be the star of the show from start to finish. Sometimes he turns things completely upside down so that what is happening does not make sense to me at all! I'm forced to cling to him and rest in his peace that passes understanding.

You may find yourself in the middle of circumstances that don't make sense to you. You may be surrounded by people who would never be your choice. Possibly God is reminding you that "the battle is the Lord's" and the way he wins battles is often through people and events we'd never even think of, much less choose. Oddly enough, that knowledge takes the pressure off of me. I can quit striving, plotting, maneuvering. I am not the star of the show; God is. That brings me outrageous peace.

© MARILYN MEBERG

When I was twenty-two I knew so much. Now at forty-two I know very little. But the very little I know now is worth more to me than all the stuff I used to think was important. I know that not a moment of my life is wasted if I'll offer it up to God. I don't have tidy answers anymore for all the heartache that's in the world, but when I try to view life with an eternal perspective, I find hope even in the darkest corners.

I refuse to get caught up in the spirit of despair that is seeping through the world and creeping into the church. We look at world events, the economy, the chaos, and we become filled with fear of the days that lie ahead, as if God hadn't read the latest edition of *Time* magazine before he gave us his Word. But no matter what is going on around us, God is in control. He has not fallen off his throne and never will. Every moment of our lives is planned by God. He makes no mistakes.

SHEILA WALSH

Promises About God's Sovereignty

"*I am the Alpha and the Omega,*" Jesus says, "*who is, and who was, and who is to come, the Almighty.*"

 Revelation 1:8

The earth is the LORD's, and everything in it, the world, and all who live in it.

 Psalm 24:1

Christ is the image of the invisible God, the first-born over all creation. For by him all things were created: things in heaven and on earth, visible and invisible, whether thrones or powers or rulers or authorities; all things were created by him and for him. He is before all things, and in him all things hold together.

 Colossians 1:15-17

146

Renewed by Hope

I'm outta here! You've seen me for the last time. I'm moving. I want out. Haven't you felt like that a hundred times? I certainly have. I don't so much anymore because I live alone, and if I ran away I'd have to take me with me. (My codependent friend says that when she gets to the end of her rope, she imagines herself saying to her family, "Get in the car. I'm running away!")

There's no escaping reality, but we all try in a million different ways. Some of us sublimate, others ignore, and many live in denial. There are numerous times when living in the present is way too difficult.

Most of us know what we don't want in life, but not many of us know what we do want. Not having what we want, or not wanting what we have, leads to discontentment and despair. But I've learned that we can do the only thing that works: turn to God and his Word. He brings about real change in our lives. How? By giving us hope.

© LUCI SWINDOLL

$\mathcal{M}$other eagles feather their nests with bits of jagged glass or splintered wood. When the wee ones hatch and grow, they are pricked by the sharp pieces and decide to take a flying leap out of the nest.

On that first dizzying flight, the young ones flap their wings like crazy as they try to find a current to slow their panic. With each trip, they learn when to ride the winds and when to dip, spin, or flap their wings. They learn how to rise above the worst, to soar higher and farther. Soon they're flying!

People are in various levels of flight training. Were we not pushed into flight by our Father, we might never get beyond waiting. God sets up circumstances that push us into trusting him to hold us up. It's the only way.

In each human body resides a living spirit looking for hope. There are hurts and needs and loves. All of us need to be touched, encouraged, challenged, or inspired. And we are meant to touch each other in some renewing way.

BARBARA JOHNSON

Promises About the Renewal of Hope

Praise be to the God and Father of our Lord Jesus Christ! In his great mercy he has given us new birth into a living hope through the resurrection of Jesus Christ from the dead.

 1 Peter 1:3

By two unchangeable things in which it is impossible for God to lie, we who have fled to take hold of the hope offered to us may be greatly encouraged. We have this hope as an anchor for the soul, firm and secure.

 Hebrews 6:18-19

This I call to mind and therefore I have hope: Because of the LORD's great love we are not consumed, for his compassions never fail. They are new every morning; great is your faithfulness.

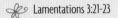 Lamentations 3:21-23

A Pink Duck Point of View

I once read the quip, "Life ain't no ride on no pink duck." It stuck in my brain like a colorful Post-It note.

One winter evening, as I walked home from my mother's apartment, a woman from Mom's building was disembarking from her car and expressed her fear of falling on the ice. I asked what I could do to help her feel safe. She suggested I take her left arm while she used her cane in her right hand. We slowly made our way across the frozen patches.

When we reached the curb, she asked, "How old are you?" I told her, and she replied wistfully, "How fortunate you are." Then she stated sadly, "But I must tell you that you don't have a lot to look forward to. Aging is painful." She turned to enter the apartment and pleasantly called out, "Happy Thanksgiving!"

When we exhibit joy during trying times, others view us as odd ducks 'cause everyone knows life ain't no ride on no pink duck.

© PATSY CLAIRMONT

God has given women the power to move on in life through the contagion of laughter. I've spent the past several years collecting quips about laughter and sayings that make me laugh. I have a lot of quotes about dieting, middle age, motherhood, husbands, wrinkles, love—you name it: all those hot spots in a woman's life that would kill us if we let them get us down. The secret is to not let them get you down. The secret of not letting them get you down is to laugh about them.

We can sigh about things, or we can laugh. Both these responses release pressure, but which is the most fun? Whatever it is probably won't go away, so we might as well live and laugh through it. When we double over laughing, we're bending so we won't break. If you think your particular troubles are too heavy and too traumatic to laugh about, remember that laughing is like changing a baby's diaper. It doesn't solve any problems permanently, but it makes things more acceptable for a while.

BARBARA JOHNSON

Promises About Our Point of View

There is a time for everything,
    and a season for every activity under heaven:
a time to be born and a time to die,
    a time to plant and a time to uproot,
a time to kill and a time to heal,
    a time to tear down and a time to build,
a time to weep and a time to laugh,
    a time to mourn and a time to dance,
a time to scatter stones and a time to gather them,
    a time to embrace and a time to refrain,
a time to search and a time to give up,
    a time to keep and a time to throw away,
a time to tear and a time to mend,
    a time to be silent and a time to speak,
a time to love and a time to hate,
    a time for war and a time for peace.

Ecclesiastes 3:1-8

Let us throw off everything that hinders and the sin that so easily entangles, and let us run with perseverance the race marked out for us.

Hebrews 12:1

Time for an Attitude Check

While traveling with a friend in the British Isles, we had a flat tire on our rented car. A huge bus had taken its half of the road out of the middle, forcing us to run into a fence, flattening the tire, and denting the fender. We managed to wobble the car down the road to a telephone and waited for the repairman.

To some this would have been a catastrophe. After all, it wasn't our car, we were in a foreign country, we had no idea how much the repair would cost, and it took time out of our day. But that wasn't our feeling. While sitting on a rock waiting, we had a spectacular view of Ireland's coastline and plenty of laughter. Neither of us will ever forget the incident, and photos captured the memory.

Why do we take minor irritations so seriously? Think of the stress we would forego if we just realized mere inconveniences can be survived. When you trust God, regardless of the circumstances, you have "life, happiness, and protection from harm" (Proverbs 19:23 TLB).

LUCI SWINDOLL

Sandi Patty, Max Lucado, Susan Ashton, and I were hosting a cruise to Bermuda. Barry and I found a cab and were soon on our way to the dock. The driver pulled up beside a lovely ship.

"This looks great!" I said. "But why are all those people getting off the boat?"

"That's the crew," the driver said. "Two-thirds of them resigned this morning."

I still have vivid memories of struggling up the gangplank dragging our cases. Then we saw our cabin. I had imagined a spacious room with a view of the waters below. But when we opened the door, I laughed so hard I fell over our bags. I wouldn't say the room was small, but we needed to take off our coats to get in. We both laughed till tears ran down our cheeks.

Each of us can choose to lose it when life doesn't live up to our expectations, or we can let it go and laugh at the funny side. Perhaps those who watch our jovial spirits will say, "Their God must be good."

© SHEILA WALSH

Promises About a
Good Attitude

A happy heart makes the face cheerful.

✿ Proverbs 15:13

*G*ive thanks in all circumstances, for this is God's will for you in Christ Jesus.

✿ 1 Thessalonians 5:18

*M*ay God himself, the God of peace, sanctify you through and through.

✿ 1 Thessalonians 5:23

I know that there is nothing better for men than to be happy and do good while they live. That everyone may eat and drink, and find satisfaction in all his toil—this is the gift of God.

✿ Ecclesiastes 3:12–13

The Curative Powers of Laughter

I heard someone say recently that laughter is her drug of choice. Simple as that. Laughter is the language of the young at heart and the antidote to what ails us. No drugstore prescription is required; laughter is available to anyone at any time. Laughter's benefits are felt immediately. With large doses, the benefits show on our face, in our body language, and in the spring in our step. So who needs a face-lift or crazy diets that don't work?

Did you know that one laugh burns six calories? Laughing is jogging for your insides. It increases heart rate and circulation, stimulates the immune system, and improves the muscle tone of the abdomen. Dr. William Fry says, "Laughing heartily a hundred times a day has the same beneficial effects as ten minutes on a rowing machine."

There is nothing like a mouthful of laughter. Get some for yourself.

BARBARA JOHNSON

When God said a joyful heart is good medicine, I believe he was literal in his meaning.

A researcher named Jonathan Leake has discovered how a group of life-enhancing chemicals are triggered by laughter. These hormones are so powerful, they can energize a person's entire immune system and help it ward off diseases, including the common cold or flu.

Arthur Stone, a professor of psychoneural immunology, has published a paper outlining the most conclusive evidence yet of a link between laughter and blood levels of immunoglobulin A. (This helps people fight illness by marking invading bacteria and viruses for destruction by white blood cells.) Melancholy people had higher levels of cortisones which are associated with stress and can damage people's ability to fight disease. Only now is the role of their uplifting counterparts, the cytokines, beginning to be understood.

God has given us a prescription for joy. All we have to do is fill the prescription.

MARILYN MEBERG

Promises About the Benefits of Laughter

The cheerful heart has a continual feast.

 Proverbs 15:15

A cheerful heart is good medicine.

 Proverbs 17:22

Go, eat your food with gladness, and drink your wine with a joyful heart, for it is now that God favors what you do.

 Ecclesiastes 9:7

A man's spirit sustains him in sickness.

 Proverbs 18:14

An anxious heart weighs a man down, but a kind word cheers him up.

 Proverbs 12:25

Jesus Gives Joy and Peace

Jesus is the one who offers us the confidence that no matter how risky life becomes or what tragedy befalls us, he will be our peacemaker. That adds to my security. No matter how devastating my fall, or even how debilitating my crash, he will be there for me. Our safety is not in the Lord preventing all our falls, but in the net of peace he spreads beneath regardless of what befalls us. He will ultimately use our slips and spills. When we fall, he helps us begin again.

This peace-producing information is especially important to clowns like me because we flub up a lot. I don't know if it's our need for the spotlight, or our self-effacing ways that trip us up, but we sure know how to stumble about, causing our peace to seem more like pieces.

But God's peace isn't fragile. Not only can't it be broken; it is powerful. It isn't the absence of problems that demonstrates peace, but being able to rest in the midst of turmoil and threat. That's when we exemplify the "peace that passes understanding."

© PATSY CLAIRMONT

Because I have so frequently used the themes of joy and humor in my writing and speaking, I'm often asked to give pointers on how to develop a laugh lifestyle. I always find that a difficult question because a laugh lifestyle is so much more than joke books, funny tapes, or humorous movies. They have their place and can certainly provide wonderful times of laughter, but the humor they inspire is external to who we are.

The development of a laugh attitude begins internally with a foundation that is God-inspired and God-constructed. Faith in that solid foundation then leads to personal rest and divine security. Without this internal peace, the laughter inspired by all the zany antics we can think of will ultimately die in the wind, leaving a hollow void waiting to be filled with the next antic or joke.

I guess if I were to reduce all of these words about developing a laugh lifestyle into one sure first step, it would be: Become personally acquainted with the Author and Giver of joy. His name is Jesus.

© MARILYN MEBERG

Promises About Joy and Peace

*L*ORD, you establish peace for us; all that we have accomplished you have done for us.

 Isaiah 26:12

*G*race and peace be yours in abundance through the knowledge of God and of Jesus our Lord. His divine power has given us everything we need for life and godliness through our knowledge of him who called us by his own glory and goodness.

 2 Peter 1:2-3

*M*ay the LORD of peace himself give you peace at all times and in every way.

 2 Thessalonians 3:16

I will lie down and sleep in peace, for you alone, O LORD, make me dwell in safety.

 Psalm 4:8

Laughter IS CONTAGIOUS

Celebrate Your Days

*A*n edict went out to offer an additional holiday to all employees. Forms were sent out for everyone to submit his or her day of preference.

Doris asked her boss his request.

"August 12," Dwayne said. "It's a Friday. I like Fridays off."

"Next year it won't be Friday. Most people want the day after Thanksgiving."

"But I already take that Friday as a day of vacation."

"Dwayne, if the company gives you the day off, you wouldn't have to take it as vacation. It would already be a holiday."

Dwayne shot back, "Then what day would I take as a day of vacation?"

Doris replied, "How 'bout August 12?"

That settled it for Dwayne.

I've laughed at this story for years. Dear, sweet Dwayne. Every August 12 I think of him. I do something different that day. The happiest people are those who are fully convinced that this is the day the Lord has made. Celebrate all your days—including August 12.

© Luci Swindoll

We Christians might look a bit more redeemed if we learned more about partying well—finding ways to celebrate the victories and milestones in each other's lives and also celebrating the traditional (and maybe some untraditional) seasonal holidays and holy days.

Families can celebrate their own events: anniversaries, Mother's Day, Father's Day. Celebrate! I know, putting on a party, even an informal gathering, takes effort, from organizing to cleanup. But I think our society, even our church, is hungry for meaningful interaction. Forget the virtual Internet party. Have a real one that includes smiles, laughter, and popcorn. Let people gather around the grill. Skewer their own shish kebabs. Make their own pizzas. Decorate their own Christmas cookies.

Why not share the goodness of God in your life with others? Gather to celebrate because we are made for community. Sign on, sign up for the party. Celebrate the moment. Set up a milestone. Treasure the memory. Share the joy.

© SHEILA WALSH

Promises About Celebrating Your Days

This is the day the LORD has made; let us rejoice and be glad in it.

 Psalm 118:24

LORD, you have assigned me my portion and my cup; you have made my lot secure. The boundary lines have fallen for me in pleasant places; surely I have a delightful inheritance. I will praise the LORD, who counsels me; even at night my heart instructs me. I have set the LORD always before me. Because he is at my right hand, I will not be shaken. Therefore my heart is glad and my tongue rejoices; my body also will rest secure.

Psalm 16:5-9

A Perfect Friendship

What a joy for two people—each to be a shady covering for the other. A place to rest when the sun is too hot or the wind too biting.

Friendship is good for your health—even your cardiovascular and immune systems. We need good friends even if we have wonderful husbands. We need the companionship of others in the body of Christ. We need other women to laugh and cry with.

When we're all anchored in the same harbor, we're able to help each other patch the holes in our boats. If a friend has hurt my feelings, I find it hard to be honest about that. But sometimes speaking the truth about a hurt is very important. When we can walk through that field with a few thorns in the grass and make it to the other side, our friendships will be stronger and our joy will be real.

Real friendship grows when we are prepared to be there equally in the bad moments and the good, when we weep with those who weep—and rejoice with those who rejoice.

© SHEILA WALSH

Friendship is the ship the Lord often launches to keep my boat afloat. I seem to require people in my life. Interacting with others encourages, nurtures, challenges, hones, and helps refine me. My journey has been made more joyous by connecting with friends.

One of my favorite friends is Carol. We are friends with history. Carol and I tell each other secrets and giggle over our silly flaws. We know the worst about each other and choose to believe the best. Since we met the Lord, our friendship has deepened in appreciation and affection. We have celebrated and sorrowed together. We have guffawed and groaned. We have worshiped the Lord and studied the Scriptures in our homes. We have at times let one another down, which gave us opportunity to learn the imperative friendship skill of forgiveness.

Differences and similarities along with years of caring and sharing have enhanced our sister-ship. I'm thankful that the Lord knew we would need each other to survive various storms—and that he made available the harbor of friendship.

© PATSY CLAIRMONT

Promises About Friendship

A friend loves at all times, and a brother is born for adversity.

Proverbs 17:17

Though one may be overpowered, two can defend themselves. A cord of three strands is not quickly broken.

Ecclesiastes 4:12

There is a friend who sticks closer than a brother.

Proverbs 18:24

Jesus says, "Here I am! I stand at the door and knock. If anyone hears my voice and opens the door, I will come in and eat with him, and he with me."

Revelation 3:20

Put on a Smiley Face

I believe in having fun, because I know that she who laughs, lasts. Whatever you do, whether it's jumping from airplanes, visiting the sick, surfing the Net, taking care of widows, or goofing off, do it well and never lose your ability to scatter joy. Tuck some in the pocket of the stranger next to you at the grocery store. Sprinkle it on the head of an elderly lady crossing the street in front of you. Leave funny messages in your teenagers' cars or on their e-mail. Wake your spouse up with the scent of roses or honeysuckle. And never ever forget to smile.

Smiles are like two-for-one coupons. Each time you let them spread across your lips, they light up the face and heart of someone else. Sooner or later a smile will come back around to you just when you need it most. And it is something anyone—everyone—can do well. Talk about a win-win situation; move over, Stephen Covey!

© BARBARA JOHNSON

We meet women who have suffered great losses and find themselves overwhelmed with grief. Women will often write to tell us how something that was said was exactly what they needed to hear. They frequently use the word "freedom" in their correspondence, signifying God's liberating touch. They speak of the freedom of forgiveness, freedom from fears, freedom from people's opinions, and even the freedom to have a knee-slapping, sidesplitting, rip-roaring, good laugh.

A dear woman had recently been widowed after thirty-five years of marriage. She was invited by a friend to attend a Women of Faith conference. She said that weekend she laughed deeply and well and couldn't believe the temporary liberation it afforded her from her pain. She began to study the benefits of a good giggle. In the process, she came across an ad for a clown school. Well, guess what? Yep, she is now a bona fide clown. She performs at hospitals, parades, and private parties.

I love that story. This woman brings healing laughter to others. Talk about freedom!

PATSY CLAIRMONT

Promises About Sharing Joy

This service that you perform is not only supplying the needs of God's people but is also overflowing in many expressions of thanks to God.

 2 Corinthians 9:12

Do not forget to do good and to share with others, for with such sacrifices God is pleased.

Hebrews 13:16

God is not unjust; he will not forget your work and the love you have shown him as you have helped his people and continue to help them.

Hebrews 6:10

Commemorate and Celebrate

Ken broke into the silence at 3:50 A.M., December 22, 1991: "Marilyn ... I must get up. You are to stay in bed for ten minutes. Then you get up, come down to the living room, and the plan will unfold!"

At 4 A.M. I got up and went into the living room. Ken had a fire, a pot of tea, and cookies on a silver tray. He had drawn one of the love seats close to the fire, lit all the Christmas candles, and turned on the tree lights. Christmas music was playing softly in the background. With happy enthusiasm, he poured each of us a cup of tea, handed me the silver tray of cookies and with a flourish of his hand said, "Eat as many as you like, Madam."

We sat in front of the fire slurping tea, munching cookies, and giggling like naughty children. I don't know when I have enjoyed a tea party more. I was intensely aware of wanting to savor those moments with my husband, and indeed I did. In fact, I still do.

© MARILYN MEBERG

$\mathcal{I}$ like having special days, days set aside to commemorate an event: birthdays, anniversaries, graduations. My journals are full of remembrances like "forty years ago today my parents were married." Or "if my father had lived, he'd be ninety today." Or, "Remember, Luci, three years ago you bought this house."

Days are important. I anticipate them. I'm looking forward to the day my friends come for Thanksgiving, to the next time I'll see my brother in Florida. And I can never quite wait for Christmas.

The word "days" appears more than five hundred times in Scripture, and the mosaic law prescribed feast days when the congregation was to celebrate by dancing, singing, resting from labor, and giving praise to God. These were occasions of joy and gladness.

I encourage you to create special days for yourself and your family. Twenty-four hours when you do something entirely different from other days ... or maybe do nothing.

This is the day the Lord has made. Rejoice. Celebrate all your days.

© LUCI SWINDOLL

Promises About Commemoration and Celebration

I commend the enjoyment of life, because nothing is better for a man under the sun than to eat and drink and be glad. Then joy will accompany him in his work all the days of the life God has given him under the sun.

Ecclesiastes 8:15

*O*ne generation will commend your works to another; they will tell of your mighty acts. They will speak of the glorious splendor of your majesty, and I will meditate on your wonderful works.

They will tell of the power of your awesome works, and I will proclaim your great deeds. They will celebrate your abundant goodness and joyfully sing of your righteousness.

Psalm 145:4-7

The Power of Words

A graphic in the electronic Scrabble game as you depart the system depicts the game board being thrown down and shattering into a gazillion pieces. I like that a lot. It feels extremely satisfying; almost as if I got in the last word.

Words can open our understanding, but words can also bring us into conflict with others. At times it's as if our opponents (husband, child, friend, stranger) have been speaking an unknown language. For we haven't understood them nor have they had a clue as to what we were trying to convey.

We need to take the time to search out each other's meanings and not treat our relationships like a game in which we rack up points. Let's not quit trying, let's not throw in the towel, and let's not walk away angry (although cool-down breaks can be helpful). Perhaps then we can hear beyond the words to the language of the heart.

© PATSY CLAIRMONT

Proverbs 17:22 says, "A cheerful heart is good medicine," and that's the tonic I receive when I read the mail. My batteries are quickly recharged with joy, and pretty soon I'm scurrying around our home with a smile on my face and a song in my heart.

After the complicated work of writing another book or an exhausting trip for an extended speaking engagement, I sometimes feel as if I've given all I can. Whatever project it is, I fling it out to the world ... and then it comes back to me, bearing strength and joy in the words of women (and men, too) from all over the globe.

The joyful letters give me strength. Here they are, able to smile once more and even share a little laughter. They have seen God turn their grief into joy—and that has become their strength. Who do you know who could use an uplifting word today?

BARBARA JOHNSON

Promises About Words

May my lips overflow with praise, for you teach me your decrees, O LORD. May my tongue sing of your word, for all your commands are righteous.

 Psalm 119:171-172

The words of the LORD are flawless, like silver refined in a furnace of clay, purified seven times.

 Psalm 12:6

The tongue of the wise brings healing.

Proverbs 12:18

How sweet are your words to my taste, O LORD, sweeter than honey to my mouth!

 Psalm 119:103

Stress Busters

My wacky, winsome, Women of Faith comrades are so outrageous. They are all clown-like in their joy-giving hilarious ways. Many times they have caused me to giggle myself breathless.

Luci's grandmother taught her that a day was wasted if you didn't fall over in a heap, laughing. Well, I have not only fallen over in a heap at these women's antics, but I've also often been reduced to a Patsy puddle as I've ricocheted from laughter to tears. Believe me, there is nothing like being disabled by a tantrum of giggles. I've learned that moments of unbridled guffawing allow one to release weeks' worth of built-up tension.

Whether we're backstage clowning or onstage sharing, our team is held fast with the glue of good humor and God's love. We have played, prayed, and praised together for the past three years as we've bounded around the country addressing hundreds of thousands of women. What a journey! And what an ongoing joy for me to be under the big top (in arenas) with these caring cutups.

© Patsy Clairmont

When I can't sleep, I lie in bed, and instead of counting sheep, I count all the fun people God has put in my life. On one such occasion, the clock on my bedside table said it was 12:30. I looked at my husband, and he was out cold.

I slipped out of bed, went downstairs, made some hot tea, and switched on the television. I watched "I Love Lucy" and "The Dick Van Dyke Show," but I was still wide awake. When the clock said it was 3:30, I went back upstairs determined to fall asleep.

That's when I started to imagine Luci, Patsy, Marilyn, Barbara, and Thelma jumping over a fence. I don't know if you've ever felt like laughing while the person next to you is fast asleep, but it makes you laugh more. I stuck my head under the covers to try to muffle my snorts.

The next time you can't sleep, thank God for all those who make your life richer. And laugh a little as you watch them try to clear the fence!

© SHEILA WALSH

Promises About
Stress Busters

Jesus said, "Come to me, all you who are weary and burdened, and I will give you rest. Take my yoke upon you and learn from me, for I am gentle and humble in heart, and you will find rest for your souls. For my yoke is easy and my burden is light."

❧ Matthew 11:28-30

Jesus said, "My grace is sufficient for you, for my power is made perfect in weakness."

❧ 2 Corinthians 12:9

The LORD will guide you always; he will satisfy your needs in a sun-scorched land and will strengthen your frame. You will be like a well-watered garden, like a spring whose waters never fail.

❧ Isaiah 58:11

Encouraging One Another

I heard a story about a mother of four teenage daughters, about the same size as she. To keep her own laundry from disappearing into their drawers by mistake, this mother started marking her underwear "MOM." Finding her dresser drawer empty one morning, she went straight to the girls. "Do any of you have underwear that says 'MOM' on it?" she asked. One daughter spoke up quickly. "No, all of mine say 'WOW'!"

Everybody has a story. It may not be as cute as this one, and it may never be written down. Not everyone will be called upon to tell their story; not everyone will want to. But we can seek out the scared, the shy, the sad, and give them a transfusion of faith so they can go on living their story with courage. There is some area in each woman's life where she deserves a standing ovation. Let's be quick to applaud each other.

© BARBARA JOHNSON

$\mathcal{E}$very day at work, home, school, and play, God presents us with opportunities to be a blessing to people who may not be as nice to us as we deserve or desire. In the middle of these opportunities he strengthens us and enables us to pay back good for evil.

It may be as small as giving a genuinely friendly smile to someone who's been ugly to you. It may be complimenting someone who is obviously jealous of you. It may be graciously offering to ease a colleague's workload even though she never offers to help you. Instead of giving those who mistreat you a taste of their own medicine, bless them. Show them the love of Jesus.

God never tells us to do anything that is impossible to do. He has given us the freedom to make choices, the ability to think for ourselves. But he has also given us a rule book, a procedures manual to guide our conduct. The great thing about the Author of that book is that he teaches by example.

© THELMA WELLS

Promises About Encouraging One Another

*L*et us hold unswervingly to the hope we profess, for he who promised is faithful. Let us consider how we may spur one another on toward love and good deeds. Let us not give up meeting together, as some are in the habit of doing, but let us encourage one another.

 Hebrews 10:23-25

*J*esus said, "Love one another. As I have loved you, so you must love one another. By this all men will know that you are my disciples, if you love one another."

 John 13:34-35

*D*ear friends, since God so loved us, we also ought to love one another. No one has ever seen God; but if we love one another, God lives in us and his love is made complete in us.

 1 John 4:11-12

A Mother's Legacy

My mother had a way of making Scripture very practical, and it proved life-changing. For example, she held tremendous hope for all three of her children, and her hope came straight from Scripture. While Babe and Orville and I fought over baseballs, household chores, and who ate the last Popsicle, Mother was praying about our futures. She was believing God's promise that our various gifts would give us opportunities to minister to people. Her hope for that outcome wasn't in her children; her hope was in God's faithfulness to his Word.

Mother had two sons and gave them both to the ministry of Jesus Christ. She supported them with monetary gifts. She prayed for them. Today, both of my brothers are in Christian work, and have been all their adult lives. They minister to everyone. Scripture promised it. Mother believed it. God brought it to pass. She was serious about hoping in Christ, and her prayer life proved it.

© LUCI SWINDOLL

I think of kids as people who spread peanut butter, measles, and happiness. They start out as babies, totally dependent on you, the lucky parents, for everything from food to love. Then they end up as teenagers, old enough to dress themselves at last—that is, if they could just remember where they dropped their clothes. How is a mom supposed to know how to relate to these fluctuating personalities?

I think raising little ones is like looking in a mirror: We get the best results when we smile. Grin more, not less. Lighten up. Let stuff go. Do what you do well and leave the rest to God.

Seize the day, the hour, the moment, and celebrate your children! After all, you have a treasure at your dining table, in front of the TV, or attached to those headphones. Always be your kids' biggest fan. Cheer your kids on. Then remember, the best way to proceed through the parenting process is pray, "Dear Lord, please put your arm around my shoulder and your hand over my mouth."

© BARBARA JOHNSON

Promises About Parenting

*T*rain a child in the way he should go, and when he is old he will not turn from it.

🌼 Proverbs 22:6

*F*ix these words of [the LORD] in your hearts and minds; tie them as symbols on your hands and bind them on your foreheads. Teach them to your children, talking about them when you sit at home and when you walk along the road, when you lie down and when you get up. Write them on the door-frames of your houses and on your gates, so that your days and the days of your children may be many in the land that the LORD swore to give your forefathers, as many as the days that the heavens are above the earth.

🌼 Deuteronomy 11:18-21

Fearless Friends

I see so much courage in my friends. Barbara Johnson is a visible testament to courage. Her head is held high, and her gaze is fixed on Jesus.

Luci loves life. She shows up soaked to the skin in the grace and mercy of God because she takes risks, she loves lavishly.

Marilyn Meberg gives us a picture of a heart with a zipper down the middle, and she chooses to live out of the half that loves God more than she loves herself.

Patsy Clairmont makes us laugh till our sides ache. She tells us that, when it seems as if our path took a wrong turn, we should take a second look. In that diversion is a gift of grace.

Thelma Wells is honest, vulnerable, encouraging, warm, hopeful, and joyful.

And I'll let you in on a secret: All the things that rest within my dear friends reside in you. Gather up your soul and determine that in Christ you will be a woman of courage, a woman of conviction, a woman of faith.

© Sheila Walsh

I love the dot-to-dot concept of people being involved with other people. I confess some dots are more my kind of dots than others. For instance, I'm drawn to exclamation points, like the Women of Faith gals. Working and traveling with these dynamic dots is truly a joyous experience.

Since I live in Michigan and Luci, Marilyn, and Barbara live in California, staying connected with them takes some effort. We share sporadic phone calls and squeeze in mail whenever we can. Sometimes when I'm talking to Marilyn on the phone, she'll pass along information for me to give Luci and Barbara, and vice-versa. Occasionally we have a conference call, which is a hoot. Picture four loquacious women all trying to say something vital at the same time.

We four also go out of our way to share jokes, cartoons, and funny happenings with each other because we know how intense life gets, and we need joy breaks, things to give us courage for the days ahead. There is nothing sweeter than to have friends who share in your joy.

PATSY CLAIRMONT

Promises About Courage

The LORD himself goes before you and will be with you; he will never leave you nor forsake you. Do not be afraid; do not be discouraged.

Deuteronomy 31:8

Though I have fallen, I will rise. Though I sit in darkness, the LORD will be my light.

Micah 7:8

The LORD is my light and my salvation—whom shall I fear? The LORD is the stronghold of my life—of whom shall I be afraid?

Psalm 27:1

We will not fear, though the earth give way and the mountains fall into the heart of the sea, though its waters roar and foam and the mountains quake with their surging.

Psalm 46:2-3

Sharing Snickers & Giggles & More

Les was at home to give out Halloween treats. That evening he received a dinner invitation, which meant he didn't hand out the bags of goodies he had purchased earlier that day.

We would both look like bloated goats if I didn't get rid of the mountainous candy stash. So one day, as I headed out the door, I filled my pockets with Snickers bars. I had to do some errands in town, and everywhere I went I handed out these miniature candy bars. To friends, to strangers, to salespeople, to women, to children, to men. Without exception they not only were surprised by an unexpected treat, but they all also snickered. Something about the gift caused them to pause, smile, and release a little giggle.

What started initially as a way around my own undisciplined appetite ended up as a reminder for me of how little it takes to brighten a day and a countenance. I had given some people permission for one moment to take a break from the rigors of life and lighten up.

© PATSY CLAIRMONT

It seems we're all hard up for a laugh. Laughter sells. Giggles sell. Tickles and tee-hees are what we all want. Tune into the toy market. Turn on the TV. As our world grows darker and more despondent, more violent, more at odds with our ideals, we turn to manufactured laughter to cope. It gets us through tedious days, lonely evenings, and now, it seems, even playtimes.

In the old days, people said that the only fun we have is what we make ourselves. And old-timers got creative to make it happen. Today we have store-bought games, hours of sitcoms filled with suggestive jokes followed by canned guffaws, and, for the little ones who haven't learned from us about real belly-busting laughter, we have Tickle-Me Elmo dolls.

What happened to rubbing shoulders and slapping knees and creating an evening of warm hilarity based on our fellowship with each other? Have we forgotten how to be silly?

Laughter is contagious. Seek out ways to make your friends and family smile. We're all desperate for the good medicine of laughter.

© BARBARA JOHNSON

Promises About Giving to Others

*M*en will praise God for the obedience that accompanies your confession of the gospel of Christ, and for your generosity in sharing with them and with everyone else.

 2 Corinthians 9:13

I pray that you may be active in sharing your faith, so that you will have a full understanding of every good thing we have in Christ.

Philemon 6

I was young and now I am old, yet I have never seen the righteous forsaken or their children begging bread. They are always generous and lend freely; their children will be blessed.

Psalm 37:25-26

Hand Out Some Laughter

What does it take to make you unplug from your intensity and giggle? A child's antics? A pet's predicament? An unexpected note? A rainbow? A bumper sticker?

Barbara is Queen of Bumper Stickers. She has a collection of fun-filled sayings that folks from all over the country have sent to her, and when she shares them in her talks, audiences just hoot. These quips succinctly capture some aspect of our lives in unexpected ways. The bumper stickers kind of zing us, and for a giggly moment we get a reprieve from life's crowded highways.

Sometimes I delay offering a gift until I can afford just the right thing, when often the right thing is as affordable as a phone call, a card, a song, a poem, or a Snickers. I think we should declare today Snickers Day. C'mon, girls, load up your purses, briefcases, and tote bags with candy bars for others and let's go on a Snickers toot. Betcha faces will light up, and instead of sighs, for one brief moment you'll hear the joyful sound of giggles.

© PATSY CLAIRMONT

Something about handmade things brings serenity. They represent more than tedious hours or backbreaking work. I think they are to our souls what water is to a fish—the context in which to thrive.

Would Martha Stewart agree? She's a woman who knows how to use her hands. The problem is, when I try to copy Martha's style, I end up with one nerve left ... and someone is bound to get on it! Wanting a Currier and Ives holiday, I end up with "As the World Turns." If you show me a woman whose home is always ready for company, I'll show you a woman who is too tired to entertain.

I want the handmade life but fall far short of soulful serenity. While Martha Stewart excels in the work of her hands, we can't all be Marthas, making candles from scratch, weaving our own baskets, or mixing our own dyes. But we can spread hope with a hand around a shoulder, a willingness to pick up someone who has fallen down, or a smile and a thumbs-up sign. And that's far more important work.

BARBARA JOHNSON

Promises About Helping Hands

Each one should use whatever gift he has received to serve others, faithfully administering God's grace in its various forms ... so that in all things God may be praised through Jesus Christ. To him be the glory and the power for ever and ever.

 1 Peter 4:10-11

Those who have served well gain an excellent standing and great assurance in their faith in Christ Jesus.

 1 Timothy 3:13

He who gives to the poor will lack nothing.

 Proverbs 28:27

A generous man will prosper; he who refreshes others will himself be refreshed.

 Proverbs 11:25

Make Someone Happy

What makes you laugh? We all have a slightly different sense of humor; different things are funny to different people. Drag out the books and jokes that make you chuckle. Tune into people wherever you meet them who make you smile.

When's the last time you made someone laugh right out loud? That ability is built into every one of us, just in different ways. We have to relax. Remind yourself to loosen up. Try not to take everything so personally or so seriously. Lighten up. Chill.

Once you loosen up, let yourself be who you are: the wonderful, witty woman whom God will use to encourage and uplift other people. You're entering a new dimension of joy that will enable you to rise above your circumstances and bring someone else with you. Catch yourself being funny. Challenge yourself to make even the most sour person grunt out a small chuckle or at least turn up the corners of her mouth. It's a great day to laugh. Go for it.

BARBARA JOHNSON

 *E*ighty-year-old Mrs. Davidson falls into the frozen-lip category. As a child, I loved dropping in on her. Mrs. Davidson was always puttering around outside doing various little chores. I liked her animals and loved the smell of her few bales of alfalfa, but more than that, I wanted to make her laugh.

For at least a month I tried every conceivable thing I could think of to make Mrs. Davidson laugh. No response. Then one day, I was attempting to perfect my imitation of Mr. Brownell. Mr. Brownell had the most memorable walk I'd ever seen. His head moved in perfect rhythm to all his disjointedness. It was quite a feat. My efforts were interrupted by the sound of what could be likened to a donkey's braying. Mrs. Davidson was laughing.

I still find myself wanting to make people smile or laugh when experiencing a gloomy waitress, bank teller, store clerk, or any other frozen-lipped personage. Scripture states that we are to be encouragers and to meet other's needs. What a fun way to take that verse seriously.

© MARILYN MEBERG

Promises About Making Others Happy

*L*et us not become weary in doing good, for at the proper time we will reap a harvest if we do not give up.

Galatians 6:9

*E*ach of us should please his neighbor for his good, to build him up.

Romans 15:2

*I*f a man's gift is prophesying, let him use it in proportion to his faith. If it is serving, let him serve; if it is teaching, let him teach; if it is encouraging, let him encourage.

Romans 12:6-8

*I*f you want your neighbor to know what Christ will do for them, let the neighbor see what Christ has done for you.

Houston Times

The Kindness Factor

What a memorable time we had at Rockefeller Center. I stood rinkside, a part of a scene I'd seen many times on television but never experienced personally. I soon found myself the official photographer for scores of people on the ice, many of whom were skating for the first time and almost all of them from places other than New York. One woman from Alabama who was so exhilarated by her unexpected abilities shouted over to me: "Get a shot of this now!" I got a perfect shot of her posterior just seconds before it hit the ice. She was immediately surrounded by gloved hands that pulled her to her feet. Laughing, she called over to me, "Hope you got that one!"

What was the ingredient that so infused the whole experience with irrepressible joy? A spirit of caring, kindness, and consistent support. Everyone cheered everyone on. It behooves us to extend our hand to each sister who slips and slides her way past us in life. She needs us. And before very much time passes, we'll need her.

© MARILYN MEBERG

*E*very one of us has felt the nudge to write someone a letter or note. Many times we don't follow up on it; we tell ourselves it wouldn't matter anyway. When we think this way, we miss giving and receiving splashes of joy.

Why not clear out a drawer in your kitchen and fill it with stationery, pens, and fun stickers? In between clean-up jobs or while you're watching the potatoes bake, you can jot a little love letter to someone. A few words are all it takes.

If you know someone who is going through a long-term sorrow, pre-address and stamp some envelopes so it's easy to jot a thought and drop it in the mailbox once or twice a month.

Someone you know is crossing a desert in her life and can use a drink of cold water. Take up your pen! In the deserts of life, hearts shrivel up. We can't let others dehydrate from neglect. Be a joy germ and find your own unique way to share a word of encouragement today. Someone you know needs it!

© BARBARA JOHNSON

Promises About Kindness

Jesus said, "If anyone gives even a cup of cold water to one of these little ones because he is my disciple, I tell you the truth, he will certainly not lose his reward."

 Matthew 10:42

When the kindness and love of God our Savior appeared, he saved us, not because of righteous things we had done, but because of his mercy.

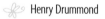 Titus 3:4-5

The greatest thing a man can do for his heavenly Father is to be kind to some of His other children.

Henry Drummond

Relative Mentors

Lots of us don't relate well to our relations. Recently my cousin Ann, whom I had not heard from since we were children, contacted me. What a surprise, and how tickled I was to learn she wanted to reconnect after all these years. (We were raised in different states, and our life journeys never had occasion to intersect.)

Ann said she woke up one day and realized she had lost contact with her father's (my uncle's) family. Now in her sixties, she decided to call all of her first cousins and to reestablish relationships. I couldn't have been more pleased, and so we agreed to meet up at one of my conferences in the south. Our reunion was fun and allowed us to reestablish our family connection.

Isn't that what connecting is really all about—being like family? What a beautiful picture of celebrating another's blessings.

© Patsy Clairmont

$\mathcal{M}$y great-grandfather, Daddy Harrell, and I became best friends. One of our favorite after-school games was "prayer meeting." The old sofa was the pew, and a tall-backed chair was the pulpit. Together, Daddy Harrell and I sang the old, metered hymns of the church. His slightly off-key baritone wavered alongside my loud, childish voice. Together we belted out songs and prayed down fire and brimstone in our make-believe church.

When I think of Daddy Harrell, I feel love all over. His tolerance, patience, and most importantly, his presence was like that of God. God knew that those play prayer meetings would be so engraved in my heart I would transfer praying into a lifelong activity and into the lives of my children and grandchildren.

Perhaps you've had somebody who lived before you the truth of God. Maybe you haven't. But you can become that person to someone you care about. All you have to do is live your life of faith for your loved ones to see. Take them by the hand and lead them to spiritual safety.

© THELMA WELLS

Promises About Mentors

Imitate those who through faith and patience inherit what has been promised.

 Hebrews 6:12

When his father-in-law saw all that Moses was doing for the people, he said, "What is this you are doing for the people? Why do you alone sit as judge, while all these people stand around you from morning till evening?"

Moses answered him, "Because the people come to me to seek God's will. Whenever they have a dispute, it is brought to me, and I decide between the parties and inform them of God's decrees and laws."

Moses' father-in-law replied, "What you are doing is not good. You and these people who come to you will only wear yourselves out. The work is too heavy for you; you cannot handle it alone. Listen now to me and I will give you some advice, and may God be with you. You must be the people's representative before God and bring their disputes to him." ...

Moses listened to his father-in-law and did everything he said.

 Exodus 18:14–19, 24

In His Hands

*W*hat would Jesus do with his hands to bring love to this world?

Jesus would express welcome in a handshake and offer unconditional love in a hug. He would sit and listen, holding somebody else's hands folded in his own. He would tickle a kid, carve a beautiful piece of wooden furniture. If this kind of handmade love is freely given in a home, Jesus' presence will be felt there.

Use your hands to express humor, articulate a joke, elaborate a funny story. I used my hands for fun times when I was raising my four boys. From Jell-O fights to backyard baseball games, humor reminds children that adults can let down their guard.

God gave us hands to give and to receive his blessings. At the table, bless the food and the hands that prepared it. At bedside, fold your hands to pray. Use them lifted in worship. At the end of the day, put your hands to rest for work well done.

We are the hands of Jesus in this world. And that's important.

Barbara Johnson

Promises About God's Hands

I am the LORD, your God, who takes hold of your right hand and says to you, Do not fear; I will help you.

Isaiah 41:13

If the LORD delights in a man's way, he makes his steps firm; though he stumble, he will not fall, for the LORD upholds him with his hand.

Psalm 37:23-24

I am always with you, LORD; you hold me by my right hand.

Psalm 73:23

Sources

Clairmont, Patsy, Barbara Johnson, Marilyn Meberg, Luci Swindoll, Traci Mullins. *Joy Breaks*. Grand Rapids, MI: ZondervanPublishingHouse, 1997.

Clairmont, Patsy, Barbara Johnson, Marilyn Meberg, Luci Swindoll, Sheila Walsh, Thelma Wells, Traci Mullins. *Extravagant Grace*. Grand Rapids, MI: ZondervanPublishingHouse, 2000. *Outrageous Joy: The Life-Changing, Soul-Shaking, Truth About God*. Grand Rapids, MI: ZondervanPublishingHouse, 1999.

Clairmont, Patsy, Barbara Johnson, Marilyn Meberg, Luci Swindoll, Sheila Walsh, Thelma Wells, Janet Grant, *Overjoyed!* Grand Rapids, MI: ZondervanPublishingHouse, 1999. *We Brake for Joy!* Grand Rapids, MI: ZondervanPublishingHouse, 1998.

Johnson, Barbara. *Boomerang Joy: Joy That Goes Around, Comes Around*. Grand Rapids, MI: ZondervanPublishingHouse, 1998.

Walsh, Sheila. *Bring Back the Joy*. Grand Rapids, MI: ZondervanPublishingHouse, 1998. *Honestly*. Grand Rapids, MI: ZondervanPublishingHouse, 1996.